31 Cents to 43 Countries

31 Cents to 43 Countries

HARDCORE TIPS TO INCREASING PROFITS

Dr. Dina Preston-Ortiz
With Don Ortiz

DEO Publishing

DEO Entertainment Group 18662 W. San Ricardo Drive Goodyear, Az 85338 deoentertainmentgroup@gmail.com ISBN-13: 9781733329811

Ordering Information:
Quantity sales. Special discounts are available on quantity purchases by corporations, associations, and others. For details, contact the publisher at the address above.
Orders by U.S. trade bookstores and wholesalers. Please contact: DEO Entertainment Publishing at: 623-330-0267

This book is dedicated to our son, family, musicians and all those serving, who have served and will serve in the U.S. Armed Forces and in foreign government posts with the U.S. State Department. It has been a privilege to serve you.

Disclaimer

T he authors of this book have tried to recreate events, locales, and conversations from our memories of them. To maintain their anonymity and privacy in some instances, we have changed or removed names of individuals, groups, and places. We may have changed some identifying characteristics and details such as physical properties, events, occupations, and places of residence.

Although the author and publisher have made every effort to ensure that the information in this book is correct at press time, the author and publisher do not assume, and hereby disclaim, any liability to any party for any loss, damage, or disruption caused by errors or omissions, whether such errors or omissions result from negligence, accident, or any other cause.

Your Free Bonus Gift

A s a thank you for purchasing our book, Don and I want to offer you access to our favorite **Top Ten Hardcore Tips to Increase Profits.** (http://deospeaks/publications/)

This free download shares the specifics of "why and how" to increase profits using our favorite top ten management, marketing, and business strategy techniques exclusive to our readers.

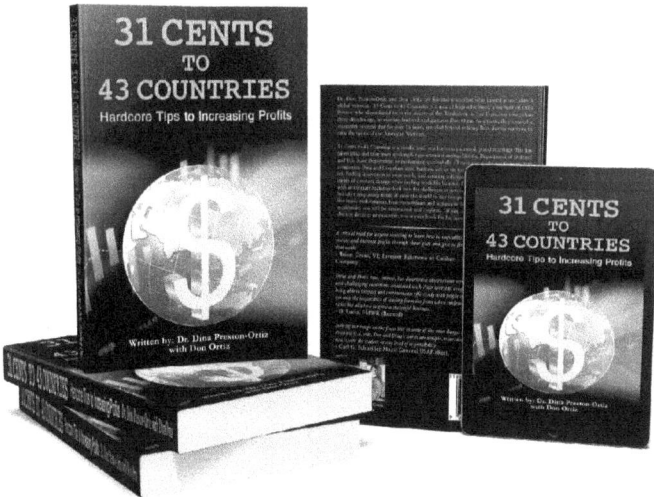

Contents

Foreward

Often, when I am asked to give my opinion on something, I have to remind those asking that there is much more behind an opinion than just words. An opinion can sometimes be viewed as an endorsement. In this case, I am happy to give my opinion as well as my endorsement. This book will not only be an entertaining and enlightening read, but also, anyone who wants to learn how to operate, outside the box, in the worldwide entertainment industry or in a global business will surely find unique gems of information in each chapter.

The entertainment business is often called a closed industry. That's because professional techniques used to produce live shows are, in many ways, unique to the folks putting on the show. These techniques are more than trade secrets, they are the result of decades of winning and occasionally losing, of succeeding and failing. But for the wise, successful business person, every loss is a lesson and, when applied, you never lose again. What you can learn from this book is that if you're willing to work hard, are willing to tell the truth about every step of every aspect of every deal, and learn from your losses, not only will you succeed in business, you will flourish.

Dina and Don have accomplished what few have. They have presented shows all over the world for people who are not simply members of the general public but also for presidents, ambassadors, generals, and others whose scope of duties cannot even be imagined. When these folks want entertainment, they call real pros, those upon whom they can trust and depend. That's the only way they operate, and that's why they call Dina and Don.

As a result of reading this book, you will learn and benefit from the experiences that Dina and Don write about with great affection. You will learn about things you never dreamt of. You will hear stories that will make your eyebrows hit your forehead. But most of all, you won't want to put this book down.

As I begin my 48th year in the global entertainment industry, I can guarantee that if you want to learn about the inner thinking and successful strategies of two people who beat all the odds and who are as passionate about their work today as they were the day they first started, this is the book for you.

John Regna -World Entertainment Associates of America, Inc. www.WorldEntertainment.net

Introduction

For the last 30 years, my husband Don and I have had a front row seat to American history. While we are not famous musicians or global diplomats, we have had the good fortune of experiencing more than our share of exceptional experiences. Through these experiences, we have gained valuable insight that offers the business community something extraordinary.

Without a record deal or artist management, we have performed with our band in 43 countries on 26 world tours. We have worked for the United States Department of Defense Armed Forces Overseas Shows and on behalf of the U.S. State Department, performing and speaking on their statecraft initiative for various U.S. Embassies around the world as Ambassadors of Goodwill. Along with our global performances, we continue to successfully work in the *Meetings and Event Industry* performing for Fortune 500 companies.

Our story is valuable because it gives a different perspective on effective business strategy. In today's turbulent and politically tense global markets, our business insights have never been more relevant in helping to take advantage of and solve real problems in business, at home and abroad.

As an adult reentry student and daughter of a first-generation college graduate, I know firsthand the precious gift of knowledge coupled with exceptional life experiences in transforming the lives of those willing to learn, along with their families and communities. Don and I continue to be inspired by lifelong learning. We are grateful and feel privileged to be able to serve our community as business owners, musicians, and educators. We hope you will enjoy our worldwide journey while learning comprehensive business insights and applications.

Part One: Guts & Grit

*"All our dreams can come true if we have
the courage to pursue them."*
-Walt Disney

CHAPTER 1

Finding Your Internal Compass

My brother always refers to my leaving home at the age of eighteen as the time I ran away with a musician. In truth, I left Phoenix for San Francisco to go to college, play music, and find adventure. Following your heart through the unknown can be a frightening experience. It can also lead you to learn new skills and open opportunities you never knew existed. In business, being authentic and true to your internal compass can take you beyond what facts alone may be telling you. By facing my fears, becoming aware, and using new information to help solve simple to complex problems, I unknowingly gained advantages in competitive business environments of constant change.

Halfway from Nowhere

The hotel smelled like urine and Clorox. With each step I took, my feet stuck to the matted lobby carpet as I headed straight for the man seated behind the glass window.

"How much for a room?" I asked through the protective glass barrier.

The man, with an obvious hangover, pointed to the sign above him and said gruffly through the intercom, "weekly or monthly?"

I looked at the sign and held up my index finger, "one month," I replied.

After taking my money through the metal drawer, he pushed out a receipt and paper outlining the house rules. *Front doors lock at 10 pm, and NO visitors past the front lobby* it said in large bold type. In my pleated, red and black plaid, Catholic school girl skirt, oversized sweater, and knee-high boots, he buzzed me in. As I walked up the four flights of stairs to my assigned room, I made up my mind I was going to be okay.

In the 1980s, the Tenderloin was home to addicts, homelessness, and hardships. It was an unforgiving place with high levels of desperation. As an eighteen-year-old female, it was a dangerous place to land. Still, from the alley window in my hotel room, I learned the art of survival at its most basic level. I watched people find food in unlikely places. I learned how to stand up for myself and when to walk away by watching back alley street fights that often took place when two or more people were struggling over limited resources. There was also hope, kindness, and prayers down the street at the local mission. Street artists beautifully expressed themselves through colorful and vibrant wall graffiti. I was now living in the rough belly of an otherwise vibrant city.

"Hey, you got any money?" the good-looking, green-eyed teen asked, leaning against the outside wall of my new resident hotel located uptown on Polk Street.

"No," but I offered him my apple with a flick of my wrist, which I'd brought from the dining hall for my walk down to my part-time job on the wharf.

"What am I going to do with an apple, do I look hungry?" he said in a snarky voice. I had to admit he didn't; if he hadn't asked me for money, I would not have guessed his position in life. At first glance, in his forest green polo shirt that matched his cool and vacant eyes, stone washed jeans and Docker topsiders, it was hard to tell he was already working the streets.

I adapted to living downtown and eventually moved from the Tenderloin to Polk Street, an early San Francisco gay community bustling with young male runaways trying to make a living on every corner. I made friends with many who were close to me in age. In turn, they showed me the ropes of getting around the city by the bay.

I made it through seedy living conditions by trusting my instincts and staying focused. Though not perfect, it was clean, and I was safer living on Polk Street than in the Tenderloin. I continued to find odd jobs and save money. Finally, I was able to rent a room near the mission district. With a stable place to live, I enrolled in City College.

San Francisco Street Musician

I kept toying with the idea of following my heart and playing music for a living. I had a part-time job at Pier 39 in a camera shop, but I wanted to sing professionally. When a music companion suggested that we busk or perform on Fisherman's Wharf between college classes to support ourselves, I was in.

Seems easy enough, right? Go to the wharf, pick a spot, open your guitar case, and play. However, busking on Fisherman's Wharf for money is both an art and a business strategy. Today there are programs in place to help regulate street performing, but in the 1980s it was crude. First, the best spots, like the cable car turnarounds, were already taken by artists who guarded them aggressively because of the daily exposure to thousands of people waiting to ride the historic cars. The dollars and coins dropping into guitar cases added up quickly as the cable cars made their turn around to pick up and drop off passengers. There was a pecking order, and if you didn't respect it, street artists would muscle you out quickly.

There is also a dark side to street performing. Still beginners at busking, my music partner and I decided to stay later than usual one afternoon, hoping to pick up a few extra dollars before rent was due.

Bright and sunny, Fisherman's Wharf's iconic Wheel was gleaming in the sunlight. With a warm and slight bay breeze, it was a perfect day to be performing on the crowded sidewalks. As the day lingered, hour by hour, the Wharf became empty as the sun started to set in the horizon, and the sidewalk pavements cooled off. Shops began to close, but there were still a few tired tourists shuffling along the sidewalks, trying to find that one last memory of the day. My gut told me it was time to leave, but I was so close to making rent that I kept pushing the time, staying much later than was safe. Still rookies, we had all the money from our day's earnings spread out in our guitar case to advertise our success and encourage more tips. Just as we were about to pack up our instruments, I noticed a group of little people pulling up on mopeds. We kept playing and singing, waiting for that last dollar of luck.

As the group got closer to us, I noticed their tattooed faces and heavy leather black studded jackets. Wallet chains dangled from their waists, making noise as they strutted toward us and encircled us both. While not big in size, there were so many that we froze. Pulling their knives, they sneered something at us, pushed me aside and another shoved my partner who knew better than to do anything at all. The leader stared at me, sizing me up and then laughed and motioned to his buddies they were finished there.

It happened so fast I didn't have time to react, feel, or know what to do. I just stood there in disbelief as they disappeared into the night with our money. I barely made rent that month, having to work many more hours because I had gotten greedy instead of listening to my instincts to leave. Being mugged taught me the need to trust my intuition, protect my assets, and not to show my hand.

Starting my music career in San Francisco was my first lesson on the importance of finding and following your internal compass. I learned that following your heart offers a path to clarity, aligning purpose with talent, and supporting outcomes through perseverance. Leaders, whether on the ground or in a boardroom, need a strong sense of direction and purpose to give them courage during times of adversity. In business, we often need to weigh where the risk is. Being willing to let go for the more important goal, while keeping calm and centered even when circumstances don't go our way is the foundation of understanding that success is a process.

I left San Francisco for the sunny shores of Del Mar, California, where I started my first country-rock band. A few years later my band won a regional music contest and were nominated for Band of the Year in the Country Music division by a San Diego music magazine. We were picked up by an agent out of Minnesota and went on the road across the U.S. and Canada.

Band on the Run

Rubbing the sleep out of my road-weary eyes, I squinted as I walked into the nightclub.

"Where's the bathroom?" I said out loud to no one in particular, while my eyes adjusted from the afternoon daylight to the neon beer signs that barely lit the inside of the bar. As my eyes started to focus, I could see the annoyed bartender nodding the direction to the bathroom with her head.

"Do you have any coffee?" I inquired when I returned to sit down at the bar. With tattoo arms, and her embarrassingly full bosom hanging out of her Alabama band tank top, the bar tapster was sizing me up as she handed me a cup of sludge coffee that had more than likely been sitting on the burner since last night. Hats, boots, and belt buckles, big or small, the cowboy bars across North America were all starting to look the same. Slowly the rest of the band started coming in and setting up.

"Let's sound check Third Rate Romance," I shouted to the band as I started to get up from my seat at the bar. It was the one song my new band member played well.

Every time I lost a band member on the road, we were set back. I had to immediately find a new musician who was good-tempered, a quick learner, willing to travel and had the technique to authentically play our style of music. If I lost a single band member, the band might change from being close-knit and tight to loose and musically sloppy. It was often torture, as we traveled from location to location, trying to live with a new person we barely knew, tighten up musically, learn the latest radio hits, hoping no one would notice the change in music quality.

As I pushed back my bar stool, the bartender looked me straight in the eye and said with a quick nod of her head, "Alabama," challenging me to play a song by her favorite band.

It's going to be a hell week, I thought. We didn't know the song, had no one to sing it, but I knew that if I could figure something out, I might win over this tough as steel barkeeper. I smiled sweetly and said, "Sure, later tonight."

In the 1980s our brand of California country-rock did not always do well in traditional country nightclubs. With time we understood the importance of putting our client's musical taste before our own. We began to learn new music quickly, sometimes daily, to help us appeal to each distinct group of customers we were encountering weekly. If we were successful, the clubs came alive at night with dance, drinks, and an occasional fistfight in the early morning hours. If we were unsuccessful, the clubs would empty out after our first set, and we would play to the employees. Those were long nights. The savvier bartenders would give us suggestions on how to please their customers because they understood that our success or failure affected their ability to make good tips in the upcoming nights of our contract.

Pressure, because of diverse music needs across the country, trained me to expand and modify the band's song repertoire to increase the likelihood of being successful. Working with bartenders to improve customer satisfaction prepared me to become a better broker and agent in my own right. As a result, I now seek out information about our clients and share it with members of our company's distribution chain to ensure an outstanding experience for all.

By 1989 I had to get off the road. I had lost two musicians while having at least six months of contracts that still had to be fulfilled. I landed at my parents' home in Phoenix and started putting out the word for a guitar player. Then I met Don.

Don Ortiz arrived at my parents' home in a baby blue, custom chrome, Dodge Sports pickup truck. My first thoughts were related to business. Don's truck was top of the line, so that meant he was a working musician. If he was able to afford a trickedout vehicle, he must be making good pay. Good musicians could demand good pay. He was probably a good musician. He wore black spandex shorts, and a neon yellow t-shirt with the sleeves cut out. With broad shoulders and an upper back shaped like a "V" that tapered to a narrow waist, he had a swimmer's body. He was handsome and totally rock and roll. If he played guitar as good as he looked, then he was just what we needed to keep the women in our audiences coming back for more. If women came to the club to see Don, the men would follow.

31 Cents in our Pockets

I first met Dina through her voice. I was working at Celebrity Theater in Phoenix between band gigs. The lighting director knew I was looking to go on the road to make some money and get away from my current living conditions. He brought me a cassette tape of Dina's band. The second I heard her voice coming through my truck speakers, I knew she was a professional singer. Her signature voice was a combo of Linda Ronstadt meets Bonnie Raitt and Mellissa Ethridge. I was turned off, though, because she had a country band and I was a rock guitarist. The last thing I wanted to do was play Top 40 country music.

I had just left an original metal band that played the world-famous Roxy and Whiskey A-Go-Go in Hollywood, though I admit I was making no real money. At twenty-eight, I already had years of experience performing in bands, from show bands to glam rock. Country music just didn't excite me musically, but the months-long contracts did. Dina caught my eye, too, when she walked in the room with a laundry basket on her hip in faded torn jeans, and her brother's white t-shirt, red Keds and matching red lipstick. I almost fell out of my seat but kept my cool. I auditioned for Dina's band, was hired, had two rehearsals and left for Grants, New Mexico at the end of the week. Don nailed the audition in two songs, and though my band was from Southern California with plenty of great musicians, none of them had his flair, charisma, and guitar tone. Don was an excellent performer with traits that drew audiences to him. I had sized him up correctly; he played great, women loved him, men followed, and, as a result, our band kept the night clubs crowded with alcohol buying patrons.

I was on the road with Dina and her band for five weeks, but by the time we hit Casper, Wyoming I knew the band was dysfunctional. While the band played good music and business was strong, there were no touring breaks in sight, a mistake for weary musicians already on the road for more than a year. With all the infighting, I knew this wasn't going to last much longer. Dina had something special, however. With her big, brown, onyx eyes, great voice, talent, and drive, I was falling for her. I knew we would make a great team. I gave my notice, but not before I asked Dina to disband her group and come back to Delaware with me to start something new.

When Don asked me to leave my band, it was a tough decision. On the road for about two years, we were starting to be known on the circuit, which brought steady work and income. The players, who I considered my extended family, relied on me for a job and their livelihoods. In the end, I was worn out. I'd had enough of band and road drama and didn't see any change in sight. This much was certain: I had my own brand, made my living from playing music, and I wasn't going to stop. I gave my band notice and quietly left after our last performance to avoid a morning scene that was sure to come.

Dina and I left after our last performance at "Sneaking at the Beacon" in Casper, Wyoming and headed back east. We had a little less than $800. By the time we made it to my hometown of Newark, Delaware, we had 31 cents in our pockets. We couldn't even pay the last toll road because we had gotten a hefty speeding ticket in Ohio. I immediately joined a local band, much to Dina's frustration, and picked up a few local gigs for money. She then booked her band (*What band*, I thought?) in Alaska for ten weeks for real money. I gave my Delaware band notice and Dina and I put together *our first band*. The club paid for our flights and gave us a van when we arrived in Anchorage. As part of our package, we were given a nice townhome for the band to stay in, which was the start of much better things to come.

Since I started Halfway from Nowhere, Don and I have been together for over twenty-nine years. Our global award-winning Dina Preston Band has performed in 43 countries and 26 rigorous international tours without management or a record deal. By working with the Department of Defense Armed Forces Entertainment Division, U.S. State Department and Fortune 500 companies, we have had a front row seat to American history.

Dina is now Dr. Dina Preston-Ortiz, and together we have a thriving corporation, DEO Entertainment Group. With years of national and international business experience that has taken us onto the front lines of more than one war, we have lived through conditions that were unthinkable. We have traveled through dangerous territory. We have learned from and helped countless soldiers remember home and keep fighting for freedom when they felt exhausted and homesick. Through it all, we have learned, grown, and thrived through every extraordinary experience retold in this book.

We have learned the art and strategy of successful business while keeping our enthusiasm for what we do alive. We have crafted unique ways of management, increasing profit, and making innovative and strategic choices that continue, to this day, to make us one of the most successful bands of its kind in the world. We have done all of this while keeping our relationship, family, dreams, and passion alive and well. Hang on to your hat! This is going to be a wild ride. Enjoy!

Don Ortiz and Dina Preston, 1989, Newark Delaware

Don Ortiz and Dina Preston, 2018, Luke Air Force Base
Image courtesy of Bill Slater

Hardcore Tips
Chapter 1: Finding Your Internal Compass

1. Follow your internal compass as a path to clarity, aligning purpose to talent, and supporting outcomes through perseverance.
2. With your internal compass in place, don't be afraid of the struggle. Struggle brings growth, change, and new opportunities.
3. To support purpose, develop cooperative business relationships to improve products and create value for the end-customer.
4. Trust and pay attention to your instincts; you can't always see the path that lies ahead.

#deospeaks

CHAPTER 2

Passion, Capitalizing on the Unknown

"Musicians are crazy," my dad commented as we boarded the crowded Muni train at the end of my long day of busking and his final vacation days in San Francisco. "Why do they work so long and hard for only a few dollars?" he said out loud as he held on to the Muni handle grip, swaying side to side as the tram left the station. From the south side of Winslow, Arizona and the only college graduate among his six brothers and sisters, it wasn't a criticism so much as an observation.

Marching up and down the steep inclines of the San Francisco streets like the true soldier he was, my dad took my busking workday in stride. Still, from his educated mind, he couldn't come to terms with the inefficiencies of working so hard for minimal financial gains. Dad didn't understand my passion. I knew the work was hard. I was living the dream every day. Sometimes eating on only $10 a week, a box of

Cheerios or a bowl of rice and beans fed me physically, while my hunger for songs kept my spirits focused. I didn't play music because of the money. I played music because I could not be silent.

"I can't represent you," said the 50-year-old perfectly manicured blond music agent as she took a sip of coffee and listened to my demo. I could smell the aroma of Bailey's Irish Crème on her breath as she spoke to me. She stopped the tape without hesitation. As her bloodshot eyes met mine, she continued, "Your vibrato is weak, and you can't sustain a note for any length of time. I'm surprised you're making any money at all." I was instantly crushed.

As I moved out of busking and into band performances, the competition began. I was not a trained singer yet. Being told that I wasn't ready to compete at a professional level was the best thing that ever happened to me.

After spending a few hours feeling sorry for myself and arguing with the agent in my mind, I called my friend Jeff, a local lead singer in a successful San Diego band. He gave me the name of his voice instructor, John Martin who took my call. After my audition, he assured me I would be a professional singer when our work was complete. John developed a unique technique that strengthens the vocal muscles at an accelerated rate. It is this technique that gives me my power and voice control, which I've never lost.

A four-foot-eleven bulldog, my vocal coach once stopped me in the middle of my vocal runs, locked on my eyes and told me that if I wasn't serious, to leave right now and stop wasting his time. He started the piano run again, this time pounding the ivory keys as if willing my voice to follow his lead like in the Phantom of the Opera.

I had perseverance and passion, but I needed to improve to get the best out of my talent. It's my voice that supports my life's work and income. As my vocal teacher, John Martin led the way for me to get the most out of a natural, but undeveloped talent by demanding I give him my best. I will forever be grateful.

Passion is important because it keeps you going when things are difficult. It supports the mastery of talent through focused effort. It teaches endurance as you continue to get knocked down and get back up to try again, each time gaining new knowledge with which to improve.

Like many of us in the arts, Don had a great desire to play music and perform. His longing came at a much earlier age when his parents were separating. Music not only calmed and soothed him during this time, but it also gave him an outlet for self-expression.

The Heart of a Superstar

My Godfather was a guitar player. I was Puerto Rican, by way of Delaware, so I didn't speak Spanish. Playing guitar is how my godfather spoke fluently to me. He would demonstrate the guitar chords and rhythm patterns, and once I learned the chord progression of the song correctly, he would play the guitar lead. This exchange of music created an instant bond between us. Much like Dina's vocal coach John Martin, my godfather gave me the start-up tools for my life's work.

Panning left to right around the tom-toms of my fire engine red, Rogers drum kit, I imagined I was Keith Moon of The Who. Playing along with the distorted Hawaii-Five-O theme song blaring out of my stereo speakers, my dad shouted, "STOP!" as he walked into our one-bedroom apartment full of the pounding noise. "NO more," he said after he arrived home from his long day of cutting hair at Tom's Barber Shop. In one swipe, he picked up and threw my beloved drum kit in the closet.

At eight years old, I said dramatically, "BUT Daaaad, I have to practice." "You're going to get us thrown out of the apartment," Dad replied, sternly.

Starting from scratch after my parents' divorce, Dad and I didn't have much, but he always made sure I had music in my life. While that was the end of my drum career, a new instrument showed up Christmas morning under the small decorative tree I had set up. It was an Egmond guitar purchased from Sears. I'd never seen anything so beautiful in my life. It was my new love. Like Dina, this love stuck.

"I'm taking Donnie camping this weekend," my twenty-something uncle said to my dad. When we arrived my uncle passed me a funny cigarette in the muddy, rain-soaked field, while half-naked people with crowns of flowers in their hair, painted peace signs and hearts on their faces were crowded in around us. Only nine years old, I was experiencing three days of peace and love, listening to every type of music imaginable at the now historic Woodstock Music Festival. Early

Monday morning as we were packing up to leave, I heard a soulful, searing guitar sound blasting from the stage. I didn't physically see Jimi Hendricks play because we were camping too far from the stage, but I stopped what I was doing to listen. Even at nine years old, I was transformed by his signature sound and feel.

On our way out of Woodstock, I bought a $2 glow in the dark Jimi Hendricks poster. It was my first good look at him. With my poster for inspiration, I started listening and practicing to his records daily. It wasn't easy, but my boyhood passion quickly taught me an essential technical skill. The magic to Jimi's guitar tone was all in his fingers. With Jimi's poster cheering me on, by the age of thirteen, I was able to play lead guitar well enough to join a few local bands.

The alarm buzzed loudly at 7:00 am, "Get up, Donnie," my dad turned to yelled before leaving the apartment for work.

Reaching over, I turned off the searing sound. I had already missed a week of my 9th-grade homeroom attendance roll call. If I didn't throw those covers off me and get up, I wasn't going to make it to my first-period history class and midterm exam with Mr. Owens. I didn't care; I hadn't cracked a book in weeks.

By the time I started high school, I was performing regularly in local nightclubs to make money. I started missing school because I couldn't get up in time to make it to my homeroom class. If I did make it to class, I often fell asleep on the top of my desk and ditched school by noon.

Don Ortiz, Age 10, Newark, Delaware 1970

After dropping out of high school at sixteen, I boarded a bus for my first road tour with an east coast showband. Only a freshman, my dad argued with me about leaving high school, but I was making better money as a musician than he was as a barber. In the end, he didn't get in my way. We had contracts with the Playboy Club and with the casino circuit, so off I went.

Beautiful Bunnies, full of grace, serviced the regulars of professional sports figures, entertainers, celebrities, and politicians. This gig was my first real exposure to playing music professionally. As a nod to my first musical instrument, my fire-engineered Kramer guitar was slung low around my neck as I hit the Playboy stage. I was surrounded by experienced musicians and was able to hold my own.

While experience is a first-rate teacher, I still find motivation from listening to other players I admire like Steve Morris of the Dixie Dregs. Hearing musicians that are top in their fields, at home and around the world, contributes to my own sound by developing a deeper tool bag from which I can draw.

My passion for and commitment to music saved me as a young boy and gave me my tools as a professional guitarist. It taught me discipline in a tumultuous environment that I couldn't always control. It let me bond with others who inspired me to be better by stretching my abilities.

Don Ortiz, 16 years old, on tour 1976

Finding passion through individual talent is a great motivator and key to finding success. A strong desire can strengthen and accelerate a foundation for the development of new skills that can improve long-term personal and professional growth. Passion can also lead to unknown opportunities.

Misplaced in Singapore

"What?" I heard Don say to the loadmaster in a surprised voice. "We're scheduled to fly home through Los Angeles."

"Not on this flight," the loadmaster said. "This plane is landing in Singapore in the next few hours and then is scheduled on to Japan."

As Don and the band hit the last note of our final encore song on the floating stage in the pristine waters of the Indian Ocean, we were told by our U.S. Navy escort to pack and get ready to leave the island immediately. The C130 scheduled to take us from Diego Garcia back to the States through Los Angeles was landing early. We said our heartfelt goodbyes to our new military and contractor friends stationed on this atoll in the central Indian Ocean. Then we boarded and settled in for the long flight home from our first Armed Forces Entertainment Tour through Operation Desert Storm I.

Dina Preston Band Operation Desert Shield/Storm, May 1992

The band had no visas or contacts to help us process in Singapore. When we finally landed, we noticed a pay phone outside the small airport. We kept our fingers crossed as Don called our contact in Washington, D.C. Time zones were not in our favor, but after the third try our D.C. contact finally picked up.

"Singapore, you gotta be fucking kidding me!" The Marine said into the receiver, and he asked Don to hang tight.

The salty Marine captain was trying to contact the Morale Welfare and Recreation (MWR) office in Tokyo at Yokota Air Base, the final stop of our C130 flight. He was quickly trying to get our paperwork in order. He only had thirty minutes before the plane was scheduled to leave Singapore. Without paperwork to enter the U.S. Air Force base in Japan, we were permanently stuck on the C130.

Don screamed to the loadmaster over the roaring propellers of the C130, "Don't remove our equipment pallet." The loadmaster looked at his watch from the airplane's loading ramp door and shrugged "I'm sorry, man" as he started hooking up the pallet for removal. Don called Washington again, willing the Marine captain to the phone. This time the Marine captain picked up. Our orders were faxing. As if shaking the good news out of the phone, Don held up the receiver yelling at the loadmaster, "WAIT, WAIT!" With our equipment pallet halfway suspended in the air, our orders to enter Tokyo to connect with a transport that would take us home finally came through.

The following year the Department of Defense sent us on the Pacific circuit. Tokyo was home base. For the next sixteen years, we continued to tour with the Overseas Armed Forces Entertainment Program, our final performances in Guantanamo Bay and South Korea. This opened other niche markets, including our current work with the U.S. State Department. We don't believe these opportunities would have happened without first being misdirected to Singapore, embracing the adventure and forging ahead to find a new niche in and passion for overseas touring.

To capitalize on the unknown, we've learned to start from the heart and to let our passions drive our purpose and progress through talent, mastery, and focused effort. We embrace and work through the unknown to find new avenues and niche markets.

Hardcore Tips

Chapter 2: Passion, Capitalizing on the Unknown

1. Use passion to define your purpose and evolve through talent, mastery, and focused effort.
2. Embrace the unknown as opportunities to find new business pathways and niche markets with reduced competition.

#deospeaks

CHAPTER 3

Being Purposeful

"The flight is going to be uneventful until we approach the landing," explained the captain during her pilot briefing. Surrounded by her flight crew and cargo of about 30-40 military personnel dressed in battle fatigues and carrying their seventy-pound backpacks full of armor and weapons, she warned: "When we get closer to our descent into Kandahar, the lights inside the plane will go off as we start our corkscrew descent." Little did we know we were about to experience the journey of our lives.

Don, the band, and I were scheduled to fly from Qatar to start our Armed Forces Entertainment tour that would take us into the heart of the Afghanistan Operation Enduring Freedom theater. Emergencies procedures were outlined as we all paid careful attention and strapped in for the two-hour flight.

The early morning hangar check-in after our late New Year's Eve performance in Qatar made this flight tiresome. As I awakened from my uncomfortable powernap on the red nylon aircraft troop seats, the captain's voice drifted over the plane's intercom alerting us to get ready for our arrival into Kandahar. Immediately, the laughter and talking stopped, the lights went off, and it became pitch black inside the plane. Going into mental battle mode, the airmen and soldiers became eerily quiet, concentrating on their imminent future as we started our descent.

Banking sharply to the right, the plane made its descent directly over the runway. In a super tight, circular path, much like a flushing toilet, the pilots maneuvered the C130 beast of an airplane in a spherical pattern for about ten LONG minutes. In total blackness, I couldn't see anything but, like a ton of bricks, felt the g-forces against my body as we continued to spiral down. My heart was racing as the rattle of the straps and buckles of the 42,000-pound payload strained against the metal floors of the C130. The Herculean engines were roaring, as we plummeted towards the ground. Wiping the sweat from my brow, I closed my eyes, praying the landing would hurry up and finish. With my body shaking, I held on to my stomach, hoping to keep its contents in place.

Towards the end of the descent, the pilot quickly pulled out of the turns to land the aircraft safely on the Kandahar runway. An army sergeant entered the plane from the airfield. Grabbing our stuff, the band made a quick exit onto the blacktop runway behind the incoming platoon. Except for the roller coaster landing, we had arrived without incident.

The military pilots flying into Afghanistan are highly skilled and purposeful. They are responsible not only for their aircraft but also for the lives of their passengers in active war zones. The pilots didn't let anything affect their laser focus when executing this difficult landing pattern. Like hundreds of flights before us, the C130 pilots landed us safely inside the Afghanistan military theater.

Much like military pilots, good sales teams remove distractions to stay focused so they can concentrate on the productivity necessary to meet specific outcomes. This includes cutting out non-prospecting activities, such as updating your customer relationship management system when you should be making phone calls or setting up appointments.

Being purposeful, whether in military or business combat, supports clarity in environments filled with chaos. Seeing clearly allows for better judgment. Better judgment supports performance outcomes that focus on a target result through concentrated skill and attention.

Don Ortiz and Dina Preston Band, Afghanistan, 2003

Chaotic Cairo

"Passports! Passports!" the police yelled, snapping their fingers at those of us standing on the sidewalk. Our passports had just left with Dina and some men I really didn't know. The police were headed our way. *Shit*, I thought to myself, *I don't want to go to jail or be detained*.

Dina and I, along with our band, often toured the Mediterranean region, including one of our favorite countries, Egypt. On our third Mediterranean tour during Operation Iraqi Freedom, we anticipated the commotion that would take place once we landed and headed down to baggage claim. It's always frenzied as passengers wait for their luggage because of the scores of local children who are underfoot trying to carry bags to get tipped. In those days, we traveled with more than 30 pieces of equipment and luggage. Though we were tired from the long travel, we had to collect everything ourselves or risk losing it in all the commotion.

One, two, three, four...five... "Hey Mister, I carry your bags, I help..." the kid tugged at my jacket. Wait, was that four or five? I was already getting lost in the baggage count and disorder and started counting again. One, two, three, four..."Hello," interrupted a sophisticated man in a dark blue suit and sunglasses while shooing the kids away.

"I'm Youssef, your escort this morning. Welcome to Cairo."

Youssef was the representative of the Multinational Force and Observers, an international peacekeeping force that monitored the peace treaty between Egypt and Israel. Shaking our hands, he said he had to take Dina, as the designated band manager, to another terminal to get the equipment carte approved and passports stamped. There was so much chaos that we didn't ask to see his credentials. In a hurry to leave the chaos of the airport, we just picked up our bags and followed him to the outside passenger loading curb.

After stacking the gear into and on top of his white van, he collected our passports. He then hired two guys from the parking lot to help him transport and unload the gear at the next inspection area. There was no room in the van for the rest of the band members, but he assured me they would be back to pick us up. As the vehicle drove off, I suddenly realized my wife was with three men I didn't know. They also had all our equipment and passports. Just then, the police on the sidewalk started asking bystanders for their passports.

Thinking quickly on his feet, our bass player pulled out a pack of mini Cohiba cigars and started distributing them to look busy. Without saying a word, we quickly formed a tight circle on the sidewalk to light our cigars against the blowing Egyptian wind. Perspiration, because of the heat and stress made our shirts sopping wet. Deep in pretend conversation and keeping our eyes down, the police walked right by us. Luckily Dina came back forty-five minutes later with the approval stamps and visas needed, and we left.

We made the mistake of letting travel fatigue, haste, and confusion affect our purpose of getting to our destination safely by sticking together and doing a better job of assessing the situation and risks. This situation could have gone horribly wrong on so many levels. We had to do a better job of being purposeful.

During future trips, we assigned specific roles to keep us working as a focused team. One band member would keep the local luggage handlers at bay. Two would count the gear. Dina or I would deal with the local contacts or any additional disruptions. Finally, we never let anyone go anywhere alone again. We now worked in twoperson teams.

Setting expectations as part of the larger team made each member feel valued. It directed us in individual tasks that needed to be completed to get through the airports, customs, and immigration. Being focused and determined also sets intentions in place to support a positive tone, regardless of the environment.

Dina Preston Band Cairo, Egypt Tours 1999, 2004

Bosnia-Herzegovina

"I gotta take a wicked piss," said the drummer.

"Me too," the bass player confirmed five hours into the convoy on bumpy pothole roads. Unexpectedly the convoy made a stop. *Maybe, we are in a safe location, and everyone can go to the bathroom*, I thought to myself. The bass player and drummer must have had the same thought.

"WAIT. We are not supposed to..." Don unsuccessfully shouted out, as the drummer and bass player zoomed off the bus into the open field by the road to relieve themselves. Getting out of his Humvee and slamming the door, the commander yelled at the top of his lungs to the men standing in the field relieving themselves, "STOP, DON'T MOVE. STAY EXACTLY WHERE YOU ARE AND LISTEN VERY CAREFULLY."

The commander continued firmly, "You're standing in a designated land mine area. I need you, one by one, to slowly retrace your exact steps out of the field and back to the convoy. Everyone else, get behind the vehicles."

With a gunner leading the convoy, our USO minibus had followed the commander's Humvee. Behind us, another Humvee and a final gunner brought up the rear. At 50 miles per hour, we had settled in for the long and rough ride. While technically the war was over in Bosnia, the aftermath was not. There wasn't a town that hadn't been destroyed by shells and bombs. Poverty was everywhere. Much of the rural population had moved to the city because of the wartime ethnic cleansing. Loading up in Hungary, Don and I, together with our band, had become part of a seven-hour convoy heading into the war-torn area of

Bosnia. Because of the danger, the convoy would not be making any food or bathroom stops. We all thought we were prepared with our drinks, snacks, books, and compact disc players with headphones. We were not.

Dina Preston Band, Bosnia-Herzegovina Convoy, 1998

Dina Preston Band, Bosnia-Herzegovina Convoy, 1998

Our band members were all standing in a potential minefield. While the field looked like farmland, we might see back in the U.S., Bosnia and Herzegovina still has one of the worst landmine problems in the world.[ii] One wrong step and they would lose an arm, a leg, or their lives as so many had before and after our visit. The band members froze in place. Cautiously lite-footed, one by one, with deep breaths, each of them successfully retraced their steps back to the bus.

To compound the travel challenges, band members were homesick and just tired of being together twenty-four/seven. The band members' morale had started to decline. Poor morale is like an infection that can spread fast and furious. We were beginning to lose sight of our mission and purpose, which was to serve those serving us. That is what we had agreed to and signed up to accomplish.

Don and I brought the band members together and reminded them that, while we understood this tour was challenging, we were right there with them and we were only in the country for a few weeks. In contrast, our military audiences were stationed there for a year or longer. We had a greater responsibility to be positive and lighten our audience's burdens. Our burdens were temporary.

We offered to send home any band member who felt they had reached their limit. However, Don and I were staying to do our jobs. If they decided to stay, we asked them to be positive and reach out to us for help when necessary. I also shared my encounter with a Bosnian woman I met who was cleaning the women's bathroom at the base. She started talking to me as I was washing my hands. She said that before the war, she was a lawyer. During the war, she watched as her husband and son were removed from their village by gunpoint. They were loaded into a truck and taken away as part of the ethnic cleansing. She never saw them again. While our journey was uncomfortable, we were safe, our families intact, and we really had no right to complain. The band came together, and we finished the tour successfully.

Today, Don and I have a team briefing that explains possible challenges before we set out on tour. We offer suggestions on how to deal with being homesick, poor accommodations, shoddy production, or overall fatigue. We share and model positive intentions, like staying calm and steady when turbulence strikes. Teaching our team how to set positive intentions to find purpose is a powerful practice.

War Ravaged Home-Bosnia, 1998

Hardcore Tips
Chapter 3: Being Purposeful

1. To support better performance outcomes, be purposeful through concentrated skill and attention to detail.
2. Outline specific roles to keep team members focused and on task.
3. Set, model, and offer tools to team members that set intentions to attract positive outcomes.

#deospeaks

CHAPTER 4

Finding Excellent, Not Perfection

"Sir, my electrical tester indicates that the power we've been given is faulty." Showing the commanding officer at the event the hot/neutral reverse polarity at the power source, Don only had 10 minutes until our show time to get the electrical problem solved. With a tent full of high-ranking military brass and German government officials enjoying local bratwurst and beer, waiting to be entertained, the electrical engineer argued on the other side of the commander's ear. "Their equipment is crap, and the power is fine, he said gargling every "R" in his throat.

The show at a U.S. military base in Grafenwoehr, Germany was going to start in 30 minutes, but Don was concerned. If the power was incorrect, our expensive digital gear would blow-up, and we'd be out of business for the night or worse, be sent home because we would not be able to complete the tour. No equipment, no shows, no pay.

The commander looked at Don and told him to start. With only seconds, Don had to decide to power up and risk losing our equipment and tour or take a stand and refuse. In our line of work, we don't mess with power, but the customer is always right. When working for the military, the commander is always right. Don was out of time. "No problem, sir" Don continued, "I'll turn the system on with a guarantee from you that if it blows, the base is responsible for repairing any damage so that we can move on to our next show tomorrow. The commander agreed.

Batmobile flames came shooting out of the power conditioner as soon as Don plugged the sound system into the designated power. The whole tent dimmed on and off and then went black. All you could smell was smoke from the toasted circuit boards just like Don warned. Even in the dark, we could imagine the veins popping out of the commander's neck as he yelled at the electrical engineer. The party was finished.

True to his word, the commander's team of electrical engineers repaired our equipment. We later learned this would not have been possible if Don did not carry the schematics of our JBL Eons speakers, Mackie 16 channel mixing board, Fermin power conditioner, DBX 32 band EQ and a Yamaha SPX 200 (all vintage gear now). The Internet was not yet well developed, so information on the electrical designs was not easily accessible. Along with duct tape, the superglue of the road, carrying our equipment schematics was another important backup strategy to ensure we stayed on the road working.

Decision-making on our tours is often repetitive and routine. Sometimes decisions must be made quickly and in unknown situations. That means making the best decision possible while trying to alleviate the risk. It requires coping with uncertainty. By assessing the risk of faulty power, sharing his concerns, and getting a contingency plan in place with the commander, Don was able to make a good decision with a backup plan. Focusing on what he was able to control minimized the impact.

Budapest in 48 Hours

"There are no flights going out to Europe tonight," said the British Airways ticket agent wearily. The famous Arizona monsoons were ripping through our desert skies keeping all flights grounded. "You'll have to wait until Saturday night to fly out to Hungary" he continued. Watching the countless passengers in front of me get denied a connecting flight, I used the only weapon I had to get us to our end goal of getting to our noon kickoff performance in Budapest, Hungry. Quickly pulling out our U.S. Embassy award letter, I silently shoved it at the ticket agent. He looked at the official stationery and U.S. State Department stamp and immediately booked us on a competitor's airline.

With hotel vouchers in hand, I dialed the recommended hotel. "We have three rooms left," the operator shared, but you better get here fast. I cannot guarantee a room until you are here." Grabbing the band members, we fled to the outside curb. "Stop!" I shouted at the hotel van as it slowly started to drive by. We all jumped into the already packed vehicle, squeezing between the other sitting passengers, while I barked towards the driver, "The DoubleTree, please." The band was already frazzled, and we hadn't even left the airport yet.

The smell of fresh baked chocolate chip cookies filled the hotel lobby. Never underestimate the power of food, a good shower, and even a little sleep to get a second wind. Although we had to be back at the airport in 5 hours, Dina and I knew we had a hard 24 hours of travel still ahead of us. Even with the flight out in the early morning, I knew we were cutting it close. If we had any transportation or connection issues in Chicago or Germany, we would need team members who were fed and somewhat rested to make sound decisions and keep tempers in check.

After dinner, showers and a night nap, we arrived back at Phoenix International Airport. Still red-eyed from lack of sleep, I handed the new ticket agent our passports and gave her our names. "Hi," I said as cheerily as I could at 4 am, "I'm checking in for Dina Preston-Ortiz, Don Ortiz," and tried to continue with the band members' names. She abruptly stopped me, "I need your itinerary and tickets," she said sharply. I went on to explain that we had no paper tickets, just our passports and driver licenses because we were all traveling on e-tickets and had been transferred over from our previous airline because of last night's monsoon.

"I can't help you," she said as she looked up my name, "you're not in the system," she said curtly.

"NEXT," with the wave of her hand, she was motioning for the person behind us to step up. I pressed myself to the counter. I wasn't budging. We had come too far and were too close to leaving Phoenix to be told our reservation was lost.

I locked my burning red-hot eyes on her and said slowly and distinctively, "We must be in the system, you do know about the monsoon grounding planes last night, right?" I said sarcastically. We were at a standoff.

Luckily, one of our musicians came to the rescue. He could see I was tired and at my wits end. He quickly pulled up our old itinerary number on his iPad, "Will this help?" he quickly gave the agent our flight information. She was like butter in his hands and immediately changed her attitude. We were finally on our way to Budapest. Upon landing, it was hard to keep still while Don, the band, and I stood in the aisles, tapping our feet and waiting for the plane doors to open so we could hit the pavement running. I had tossed and turned on the plane, never finding my comfortable spot on Don's shoulder. With no real sleep in the last 48 hours, we had to successfully de-board the plane, grab our luggage, and find transportation in Budapest. It was already 10 am with a sound check scheduled for noon. We had 45 minutes to pick up our bags and equipment, get to the hotel, check in, shower, get dressed, and meet our embassy escort.

I'm proud to say that we had an excellent team of musicians who took each trial in stride and worked with us to solve problems. They understood the possible ramifications of not arriving on time, including challenges for the embassy or a canceled tour. We were working on adrenaline, but we performed a successful two-hour show for the Deputy Ambassador and his guests. While not perfect, we still delivered excellence.

With team involvement and focus, we met every travel challenge thrown at us by taking ownership of what we were able to control to be an effective performance team. Effective teams are an excellent way to optimize limited resources through two-way communication, precise goal setting, and supportive management.

Don Ortiz @dinaprestonband Rockin U.S. Embassy Tour Budapest, 2013
Photo courtesy of Dmitri Tarahovsky

Optimizing Resources

Using an interpreter, Don said, "Let me explain how this works." Don proceeded to showcase the sound-board levels and features, hoping it would calm the amateur soundman down. It didn't help. Every time Don left the soundboard to move to the front of the stage for his guitar lead, the owner of the sound system started reducing the levels on the soundboard because he was afraid the band was going to damage his speakers. With a sixteen-channel mixer, he didn't understand the headroom the soundboard was capable of producing. Like a nuclear reactor getting ready to blow, Don could no longer tolerate the owner's inexperience and interference.

The outdoor audience in Sumqayit, Azerbaijan Center City, was growing fast. The local police were already pushing people back from the steps of the government building when the band arrived. Don noticed right away that the sound system was too small to cover the area and growing crowd. The small system was better suited for a DJ or an inside ballroom gig, not an outdoor concert. Don looked at the system with great concern.

Dina is right. As the soundman for our smaller gigs, I was troubled. I knew the system provided would not be able to produce enough sound to energize the crowd. In an outdoor setting, the sound system needs to have enough punch and throw so the listeners can feel the music and experience. This system wasn't capable of helping to seduce and captivate an audience.

Don made a few adjustments to the small system for better output. The owner of the system, a short, balding man in a black suit and white shirt was cooperative until he heard the band's sound check. Immediately, he started to wave his hands above his head, frantically yelling in his native Azerbaijan tongue that we were going to " onun Ötürücü partlatmaq" (blow up) his gear!

Turning his head, Don narrowed his eyes and quietly said to the State Department official, "Remove this guy from the stage. If he touches the soundboard one more time, I'm going to-!%&*#." The soundman was quickly removed.

I really wanted to do a good job, and the amateur soundman's inexperience was getting in the way. There was no way I could run sound, perform, sing, and give it my best while having a soundboard war. The amateur soundman continued arguing and being combative with the embassy official, but to their credit they got him to move into the audience to enjoy the show.

Whether it is human, technical, or capital, learning to optimize resources is important to gain efficiencies regardless of the size of the organization. By re-engineering the system and taking back control from a vendor who didn't have the technical knowledge or experience, Don found excellence over perfection. This ended up being one of our best shows in Azerbaijan with our novice soundman ultimately congratulating Don and the band on a job well done.

As essential as our equipment is to getting our sound and performance right, more important is our team of musicians and talent. They are the true gift behind any success we achieve on stage. They are the magic that supports our competitive edge.

@dinaprestonband Sumqayit, Azerbaijan, 2007
Photos courtesy of Dmitri Tarahovsky

Hardcore Tips
Chapter 4: Finding Excellence Not Perfection

1. Diagnose the problem before accepting a condition of risk.
2. Develop alternative solutions for the identified problem.
3. Define the limitations of the final decision.
4. Create a backup plan to minimize any negative consequences.
5. Re-engineer resources for value over volume to optimize resources.

#deospeaks

CHAPTER 5

Capitalizing on Talent

A re you sure they want disco music?" I asked Don as we walked to the stage for our New Year's Eve Gala performance. In their gold lamé and vintage black tuxedos, this looked more like a Frank Sinatra, Bobby Darren, and Dean Martin crowd. "Yeah," he said, indicating the room's disco theme and mirror balls hanging over every white linen table in the elegant Liberace-like, gold ballroom. Raising their eyebrows and quietly whispering to one another as they sipped their Manhattans and Gin Martinis, our opening 15-minute disco medley by the Bee Gees, Donna Summer, and Barry White flopped. This crowd, apparently in their 80's and 90's, didn't want to strut the floor a la John Travolta, they wanted to foxtrot and waltz with perhaps an occasional jitterbug. We needed a life raft and fast.

While we huddled in the back of the house where the evening's food was being prepared, cooked and plated, waiters rushed by us with platters of prime rib and lobster. On that first break, we came together to figure out how to fix this musical catastrophe.

Everything from the event theme and décor to the evening's contracted music was wrong. Our Berkley-trained piano player took the reins, mapping out the songs he thought the band could handle without charts. We collectively agreed to stay away from songs like "Satin Doll," but easily could manage "Take the A Train" and "C Jam" by Duke Ellington. With a few of our own standards added in to give the older repertoire a bit of a face-lift, we headed back with a new song strategy in place.

Sitting back down at his keyboard as we soundlessly took to the stage, the audience ignored us with disdain, remembering the music from the disco set. Tinkling out the first bars on his black and white keys...da-da-da-dada... da-da-da-dada-da, "Start spreading the news," our keyboard player began to croon in his buttery, tenor voice. Wide-eyed, the audience immediately looked up.

From frowns in set one and an empty dance floor, "New York, New York" brought the audience to its feet. Locked arm in arm, doing the can-can, our eighty and ninetyyear-old audience members were now dancing, laughing and engaged with the band. Our keyboard player saved the World Series of gigs, New Year's Eve, because we stepped aside to let him lead.

In today's dynamic business environments, leaders need to guide and make the most of their team of talent by building collective leadership. By placing emphasis on completing a task successfully, individual skill sets can be the foundation for leadership based on expertise.

To bring out the full potential of our team, Don and I welcome talent that pushes the band's musical boundaries. By doing so, we always uncover hidden capabilities that contribute to our own growth. Leveraging your team's talent yields a high return at a much lower cost.

History of Rock & Roll

I leaned back in my squeaky office chair and thought, "God, this is boring." Tapping my finger on the keyboard, I erased everything on my presentation slide. I rang Sam, our bass player who taught music at a sister college. "I'm developing an outline of rock and roll's music history for our Fiji tour, but I need to bring it to life with stories and real-world musician application. "Can you help me?" I asked.

"Sure, I'd love to" chuckled Sam.

The University of South Pacific's outdoor veranda was full of student laughter, out-of-tune instruments and students practicing the meke, a traditional dance of Fijian storytelling through song. Teasing them as we struck the first note of our song, "Get Back to You," the students from across the balmy breezeway instantly looked up. Causing them to stop their activities to bebop to the ska backbeat and tight harmonies, this happy song always has a way of bringing people to us.

Looking back at the band during the applause, I knew we had captured the audience. "Does anyone know the rhythmic feel to this song?" I started to explain the influence of Caribbean calypso with American jazz and blues rhythms as an influence on American rock and roll and our own application with "Get Back to You," the song we wrote exclusively for this tour.

"Let me show you the bass technique," Sam jumped in immediately, demonstrating the walking bass lines with accented rhythms on the off backbeat. Along with the shiny, crimson parrots dotting the open terrace's landscape, squawking in unison with Sam's upbeat movement, we were off and running. By the end of the presentation, our student audience did their own rendition of "Get Back to You," adding their own musicality and ownership to the song that we wrote to help us build relationship bridges.

By working through and presenting together, Dina and Sam provided an indepth and interactive lecture for USP music and art students. Dina developed the foundation of the lesson, while Sam supplied real experience as a schooled musician by sharing funny stories and techniques used across the genre of American rock and roll music. They were a hit and later we had some of the same audience members join us at similar lectures, music master classes, and performances given around the city of Nandi, Fiji.

In business, capitalizing on your team's talent generally produces a better outcome for the organization and client. Encouraging an inclusive manner of thinking by tuning into and bridging your talent's different skills and strengths improves an organization's productivity through shared accountability.

Dina Preston Band, University of South Pacific, Fiji, 2016

Shared Experiences

The stage lights were so hot that with every note played you could feel the heat pulsating throughout your body. The noises from the intimate downtown Fijian nightclub echoed and ricocheted through the smoke-filled air. As fast as Sam played the intro bass line to our opening number, he quickly released his instrument from his shoulder strap and ran off stage holding his hands to his mouth. Like a ground squirrel packed full of nuts for temporary storage, his cheeks were full. Something was terribly wrong. Within moments, our first song of the evening included the sounds of Sam's guts violently being expelled in the small bathroom stage right. If we could hear it, so could the audience.

While playing his guitar Don "Spocked" me with his eyebrow, "I told him not to eat the white sauce," I could hear him say telepathically. While the reception before the show was delicious and lovely, we had been traveling long enough to know that it is best for us to stay away from any kind of food that can spoil quickly. Sauces made with creams or mayonnaise fall into that category. Sam didn't listen or didn't believe us, and we were all now suffering the consequences.

With only a drummer, Don's guitar, and my voice left on stage, we hadn't even completed our first song. As the first official performance for the U.S. Embassy Suva, we had to quickly figure out a way to work together to successfully complete the performance. We were representing the U.S. Embassy, so quitting was not an option. Those of us left on stage didn't miss a beat (literally) as the drummer and Don gave visual signals to the soundman to bring in more bass on the guitar and kick drum. We did the show by choosing songs that Don could play signature bass lines in between strums, while the drummer played a bit heavier footed. Don's guitar synthesizer came in handy, but the performance was a challenge with only guitar, drums, and vocals.

While we were playing the show, the embassy personnel loaded up our sick musician and took him to the hospital. When the show was over, we immediately went to be with him. Luckily, after they pumped fluids back into him, our ailing musician was released and able to finish the tour.

The band still laughs about the drama of that performance in downtown Nandi, Fiji and we now have an inside joke about eating the white sauce. However, bottom line, no matter the obstacles, we quickly pulled together as a team. We had each other's back and made the performance, that otherwise would have been stopped dead in its tracks, work. It created a bond among our team of musicians that is still special today.

Whether a service organization like our band or a manufacturing company, shared experiences in organizations influence behavior by building a set of common values. It supports organizational culture through problem-solving because you have made it through the best and the worst of it together. As musicians who work with us know, no matter the situation, our organizational culture and values dictate that the job must get done.

Our job as bandleaders and business owners is to help steer and support the person leading the team for the moment. Letting leadership rotate based on expertise helps develop trust through attention to individual strengths and shared decision-making. Shared history supports talent development by bonding people who develop organizational behavior based on mutual values. Building a team of talent supports solid organizational performance and ultimately, happy clients!

Hardcore Tips
Chapter 5: Capitalizing on Talent

1. When appropriate, delegate authority or ask team members to participate in the decision-making process.

2. Don't be afraid to follow, letting leadership rotate based on expertise.
3. Developing shared experiences with talent helps to create organizational values that drive a positive and successful culture.

#deospeaks

CHAPTER 6

The Power of Joy

L eaning over Don to look out the window of the small commuter plane, I blurted out, "This is exquisite." A giant grin spread across Don's face. He'd been watching the magnificent view unfold from his window seat for quite a while and was glad I finally was taking notice. Below us were islands, dense with reefs, and atolls spread out over miles and miles of turquoise blue-green waters, rich with multicolored coral reefs and puffy blue clouds. It felt like we were flying into heaven.

We headed to Kiribati right after our 4th of July celebration for the U.S. Embassy Suva, Fiji, located in the South Pacific just west of the Christmas Islands. I was scheduled to guest lecture at the island's University of South Pacific with the band booked to perform in its capital city of Tarawa the following evening.

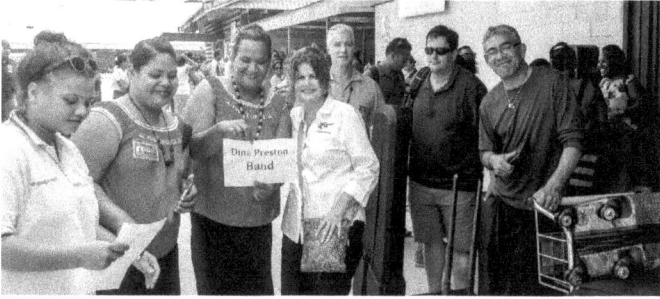

Dina Preston Band Arrival Kiribati Bonriki International Airport

As the first American band to visit this historic island, we arrived at a full house of concertgoers at Kiribati's sports arena the following evening. It seemed as if everyone from the Islanders to the archeologists (who were working to recover and repatriate American servicemen from the Battle of Tawara) to New Zealand contractors and the island's government officials were in attendance. We had a group of young talented Kiribati singers perform with us in the show and finale that evening. Born with voices from the island gods, they brought down the house.

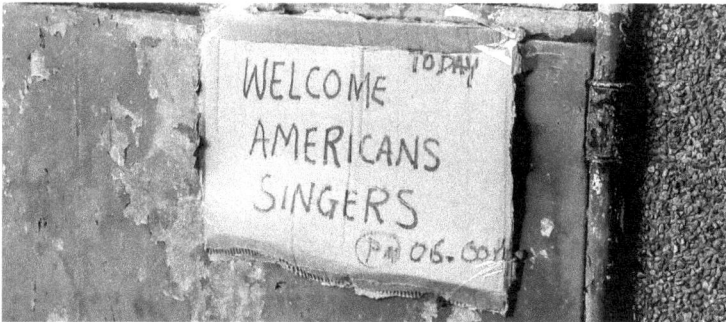

Dina Preston Band Welcome Sign, Kiribati Sports Arena, 2016

Dina Preston Band, Kiribati Sports Stadium Performance, 2016
Photos courtesy of Raimon Kataotao

Dina Preston Band, Kiribati Sports Arena, 2016
Photos courtesy of Dmitri Tarahovsky

"Let's add a show at the teachers' college tomorrow," suggested our Kiribati government host and escort as we all gratefully packed into the air-conditioned van after the center city's encore performance. It was the end of our tour, and the weight of exhaustion from traveling and the stifling heat was beginning to take its toll on all of us. The teachers' college performance was not on our schedule, but we wanted to support the U.S. Embassy's mission and our wonderful hosts.

The bass player and drummer steadily vamped on the ska beat of "Get Back to You" as Don's horns blared from his guitar synthesizer. Confident from the previous evening's performance success, we finished the song with a Blues Brothers' grand entrance forward flip. Upon landing a musical 10, the audience responded with dead silence. They were not impressed...1, 2, 1234.... I counted off the next song quickly.

"Mauri everybody, we're happy to be here with you," as I made a simple introduction in Kiribati over the vamping music, each band member did a quick musical greeting on their instruments. When it was his turn, Don moved out front. With a few performance tricks up his sleeves for times like these, he put his guitar behind his head and started playing to wow the crowd. The band ended the introduction to the sounds of night crickets. Strike two; we had one more chance to get this right.

A bit shy at first, I asked the students to volunteer their teachers for a twist off. Hundreds of hands went up, and we were off and running. The whole room exploded with laughter as even the most conservative Kiribati teacher couldn't keep their body still to the music of Chubby Checker's "Twist." The noise and laughter bellowing out of the building's shutters soon brought crowds of swarming students who stood at the windows and doors of the lecture hall to get a glimpse of the fun. You could hear the students' delight as they watched their teachers twist up and then down, sometimes getting stuck in the "down" position and falling over, unable to twist back up again. Holding their sides and rolling on the floor, the audience's tears of laughter were uncontrollable.

There is nothing better than letting go and laughing deeply to inspire happiness from within. Joy has its own healing powers of transformation. We were all having so much fun our energy levels immediately rose, and we no longer noticed the stress from striking out twice with the audience, the stifling heat, and our weary bodies. We didn't wait to let joy find us; we actively sought to create joy. Laughter lightens everyone's load.

Dina Preston Band, Kiribati's Teacher College Twist Off, 2016 Photos courtesy of Dmitri Tarahovsky

Dina Preston Band, Kiribati's Teacher College Students Outside Lecture Hall
Photos courtesy of Dmitri Tarahovsky

Man, I Feel Like A Woman

"Who's the highest-ranking officer in the room?" Dina asked the audience at Prince Sultan Airbase in Saudi Arabia. The many voices started rumbling and collectively yelled, "General Larson!" This crowd was going to be rowdy; terrific! It's always easier to bring a raucous crowd along than a shy one.

When working for Armed Forces Entertainment out in the theater, we have a habit of calling up the highest-ranking officer to join us on stage. All the officers are good sports, and their platoons love seeing them perform with us. It is the one time the lower ranking military members don't have to say "yes, sir," "no, sir," or "how high, sir?" Laughter is a great way to make it through difficult situations because it keeps everyone upbeat.

General Larsen bravely walked on stage to a roar of applause from his men. "General, thank you for joining us tonight. I heard through the grapevine that you're a performer at heart and was wondering if you'd like to sing a song with me?" The general knew he was stuck, so he politely played along and with a big smile just waited for my next move.

"General, sir" I continued, "one of the most requested songs I'm asked to sing, in fact, I was asked to sing it tonight, is "Man, I feel like a Woman. Are you game?" The crowd howled with laughter. This song from Shania Twain was crossing U.S. pop and country charts but was also platinum across the world, and everyone knew it.

With a twinkle in his eyes, General Larson said, "Let's do it!"

Prancing around the brawny officer, I held up the mic for him to sing the chorus line "Man, I Feel Like a Woman" on cue. This gruff and battle-worn officer took this women's anthem song in stride and played along as the audience held their sides, falling out of their chairs with laughter. By the end of the song, everyone in the auditorium was standing up yelling along with the general as he sang, "Man, I Feel Like A Woman." While on the surface it might look like we were poking fun at the officer, the general understood that we were helping to decrease stress and for just a moment reduce the power distance between him and his soldiers. We received emails from soldiers who shared they were still laughing at the memory of their commanding officer singing "Man, I Feel like a Woman." This morale booster broke the intensity of their mission, even if it was only for a moment. Their leader understood the value of humor in relieving tension and even loss in stressful battlegrounds. (See Appendix A, p.157)

The Frontline News
Soldiers sing with
Dina Preston Band

Casey Craig

Lt. Col. Eric Schwartz, 1st Battalion, 64th Armor commander, Maj. Michael Donovan, 1/64 Armor S-3, and Capt. Warren Sponsler, 1/64 Armor S-4, sing Shania Twain's "I feel like a woman" with singer Dina Preston and guitarist Don Ortiz during a USO concert Jan. 10 at Camp Pennsylvania, Kuwait.
Spc. Mason T. Lowery

Soldiers sing with Dina Preston Band

Soldiers took a break from training and maintaining to let loose and blow off some steam with The Dina Preston Band Jan. 10. The band brought their mix of blues, country and rock 'n' roll to the soldiers at Camp Pennsylvania for a USO concert. Rather than just sing to the soldiers, Dina

Dina Preston Band Camp Pennsylvania, Kuwait The Frontline News

Tower Theater

I could hear the red velvet, grand drape mechanism slowly pulling back, exposing us to the full-to-capacity downtown theater in Bend, Oregon. Without a single note being played, Don started marching in place with his black Ostrich cowboy boots and his tobacco Fender Stratocaster hung around his neck. With a huge American flag as our backdrop and our band logo glowing on top, Don's marching, accented with the kick drum against the stage's wooden floor echoed loudly throughout the theater. Enthusiastically, the crowd started shouting and clapping in synch with Don in anticipation of our first song. With my heartbeat in my throat, the electricity of patriotism was not only moving quickly through the audience but through me as well.

"Don, the 29 Palms Marine Corps are in the audience tonight," the producer shared as she walked us to the stage. "Can you do something special for them?" she whispered.

"Absolutely, thanks for letting us know." Don answered, "We'd be honored to..." In high spirits, I tightly hugged the two marines who were leaving center stage. Moving towards the right and left stairs that would take them back into the audience, they stopped dead in their tracks and turned to face one another like opponents in a dual. Taking a deep breath, they silently held up their fingers to the audience, counting off... 1, 2, 3. I could see the entertainment bug had bitten them. Out of nowhere, like Tom Cruise in his famous Risky Business move, the two red-cheeked marines synchronized their running start and crisscrossed the theater's stage much to the demise of their pants, which then had sizable gaping holes in the knees. The audience split their sides with laughter as these two charming comedians quickly popped back up to take their much-deserved bows.

What we didn't know is that those marines were being shipped out to Afghanistan the next morning, reinforcing how important it is to find joy by making every moment count. Some of marines didn't make it back home. As hard as the news was to hear, we felt comfort in knowing that we had provided these American heroes, representing the stars in our nation's flag's field of blue, with some joy before they left.

Scientists say that laughter releases our body's endorphins. Laughing promotes a sense of wellbeing that even temporarily releases our focus on troubles. The people of Kiribati showed us the power of real joy and happiness, not gained from material things, but through engagement and participation in life. General Larson demonstrated the importance of being able to laugh at oneself to reduce the stress, at least for a moment, of the power, distance, and intensity of combat zones and hostile elements in the theater of war. Our U.S. Marines demonstrated the courage of finding joy in the moment.

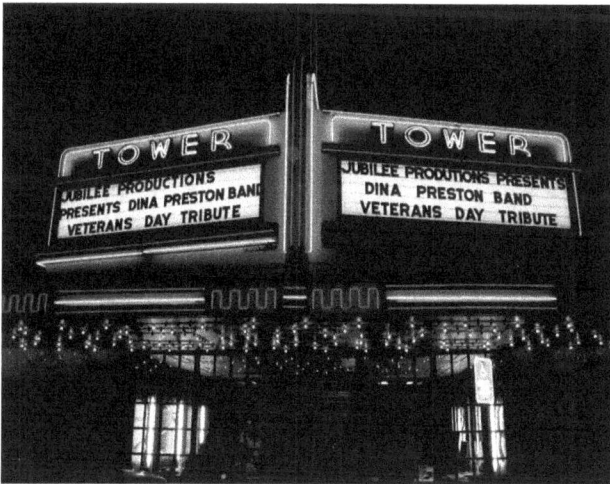

Dina Preston Band, Tower Theater, Bend Oregon

Hardcore Tips
Chapter 6: The Power of Joy

1. Create joyful encounters for your customers to build memorable experiences.
2. Don't take yourself so seriously as a leader. Learn when it's okay to laugh at yourself to break down barriers with your team.
3. No matter the obstacles find joy in the moment by being aware and conscious of your surroundings and senses.

#deospeaks

Part Two: Dynamic Disruptions

"It is not the strongest of the species that survive, nor the most intelligent, but the one most responsive to change."
                                                                    –Charles Darwin

Increasing Performance in Virtual Environments

The early morning Sonoran sun was breaking through my bedroom window and across my face. I turned over to hide my eyes, but it was too late. I was awake. Still in zombie mode, I sighed as Bella, our black and grey tabby cat licked my face. I haphazardly tried to put on my glasses, grabbing my phone to check for any early morning gigs that might have come in during the night.

Did I read this right? I rubbed my eyes several times to refocus, but there it was in bold caps yelling at me in the subject line, Re: INQUIRY FOR EVENT BOOKING IN CHIHUAHUA, MEXICO. "Don, wake up!" I reached over and smacked him on his leg. "We got a gig offer from Mexico." "Huh?" he grunted still half asleep. I read it aloud, "I'm contacting you on behalf of Sounds Records. We are a talent booking and management agency located in Sonora, Mexico. A colleague recommends your band for an event. We are looking to hire a country band for ten days (ten performances, one each day) for an event in Chihuahua, Mexico in October. We are wondering if you'll be interested in working with us." Now both awake, Don and I were ready to pounce on this new opportunity.

Located across the Arizona state line, we responded to the email request by sending a long list of questions regarding logistics, arrangements, and pay. Because the request was from someone we didn't know, we immediately contacted the Mexican Consulate to conduct a background check. When we got the Mexican Consulate involved, we stopped hearing from the music agent completely. No matter how many times we tried to call or send emails, the communication just stopped.

Bringing in a government authority so soon, like the Mexican Consulate, may have made our potential partners in Mexico feel uneasy, that we did not trust them. Relationships are important in high context cultures such as Mexico. Instead of pressing about the logistics, pay, and contacting the consulate upfront, we should have developed a friendship first. Just a few hours across the border from our hometown, it would have been worth it to go and meet the business owners face-to-face to help create these trust bonds.

Latin Americans view time as flexible rather than fixed and unmoving. Decision making takes longer, and communication is often indirect. Relationships are key in gathering information about business partners and projects. If we had considered these cultural contexts and slowed down, we likely would have found what the consulate already knew, the business and festival were legitimate. Because we were aggressive in pushing for quick answers and information due to our own pressing schedules, we lost a potentially good gig and client.

Leading in a virtual environment, across cultures, requires consistency and accessibility. We return all virtual communication within 24 hours. However, if we are working in a high context culture like Mexico or South Korea, we've learned to wait a week or two before we check back in with a client to honor their communication approach, but we are still consistent in our communication behavior.

The key when working in a multicultural virtual environment is finding a balance between the needs of the partners. Good leadership in virtual environments considers timing, communication barriers, cultural differences, and builds trust through common values before setting out to manage a task for successful outcomes.

Finding Shared Values

"Let's go look at the sound system for tomorrow night." Our embassy personnel went on to explain to Dina and me that he hadn't heard back from the island's music store in the last few weeks, so once we landed on the island, he wanted to do an in-person follow-up.

Rolling out of the white, air-conditioned van into the humid, tropical heat made this island day unbearable, even with the swaying palm trees and pristine white sandy beaches. Squinting our eyes from the intense sunlight, we ran into the music store expecting to find air-conditioning, but there was none. Floor fans were moving at high speed, spreading the dust throughout the store and in our mouths and noses. At the end of the counter, dangling a cigarette from his mouth, sat one-legged Loto, as the islanders called him. He looked at us but didn't move a muscle. I felt like we were disturbing him, but from what, I did not know. The store was silent; the only thing moving was the gritty dust being pushed in the air by the loud fan that clinked on every third rotation.

"Hello, I'm from the U.S. Embassy. I've been trying to reach you via email and text for the last few weeks to follow up on the sound system for the Dina Preston Band concert tomorrow night. Is everything ready?" our embassy representative shouted over the fan.

Loto eyed all of us, "You're not due here until next week," he said slowly. After a round of "he said/she said" regarding the missed emails and text communications, Loto sent us to a local island club to check out the available equipment.

"Do you think we'll be able to pull off the concert with this equipment?" the embassy official asked out loud after seeing spiders the size of our hands nesting inside the drums. The club had been closed for years, and we all wondered about the reliability of the sound system. With flashlight headbands on our heads like miners, we silently moved around the blacked-out club checking for quality gear. Dina responded to the embassy representative's question and gave the concert a seventy/ thirty percent success-rate.

Returning to Loto's music shop, the embassy representative impressed the importance of this performance for the island and embassy. Not only were we the first American band to perform on the island, but government officials would also be in attendance, and local musicians would be playing with us. Our embassy official was trying to connect with Loto through a common goal. Nodding, Loto held out his hand, silently giving us his promise to come through with the right equipment. We all shook hands to seal the deal, though we did show up early to sound check and mitigate any issues that might come up. The nesting spider, now the band's unofficial island mascot, came along in the drum kit and stayed for the successful show.

To combat communication differences once we arrive on island sites, we work towards developing a common set of norms and standards with our new partners by identifying shared values. Because our events are short-term, we don't have much time to nurture these relationships, so we try to find common ground with our new partners immediately. Perhaps we share a love of music, have a similar family background, or maybe it is working as a team to give an unforgettable performance. We found this common goal with Loto, he knew the importance of music to the island and as the only music store around he did not want to be responsible for any failure due to equipment issues.

We often start communication virtually and adapt when necessary. Online we negotiate agreements, decide on procedures and protocols, and promote cooperation through shared values. Finding core competencies such as excellence, creating goodwill, and problem-solving through creative approaches are all examples of underlying influences we employ. By observing and tailoring our communication style to the communication needs of our end users, we build trust and gain competitive advantage. Building relationships based on trust between generations can be challenging, however; especially with millennials who do not like to communicate using traditional tools such as talking on the phone or email.

Millennial Communication

Millennials are now in the workforce. Born between 1982-2002, they are now a significant part of the labor force and are holding corporate buyer positions, giving them power. They have the power to buy, not buy or to simply ignore a seller, or even follow through with closure. As buyers, it is not an option to ignore the effect technology has on millennials' communication choices. However, purchasing is a two-way street.

One of our long-term customers recently recommended our services to a colleague who oversees entertainment at a casino. This type of recommendation is usually enough to get some kind of response. I'm interested, I'm not interested, I'm interested but not currently in the buying cycle. After her thoughtful introduction, we followed up via email and phone. Nothing. We thanked her but let her know we had not received a response from her referral. She said not to give up and that her contact was busy, yet she knew we were a good fit for her colleague. After five months, several emails and phone calls to follow-up, the referral contact sent a quick email and said he'd get a hold of Don to arrange a meeting after the weekend, on Monday. He never followed up. Don learned later he had planned to go on vacation Monday. He had no intention of contacting us.

Our client finally arranged a meeting for herself with this elusive millennial. Don met with them, had great face-to-face rapport, and the referral contact promised to send gig dates that afternoon. We thought we had broken the relationship barrier. We were wrong. A week went by, and we were back to square one, no follow-up or communication. He wouldn't answer email or direct phone calls. We were experiencing our first encounter with ghosting, the term for the strategy employed by some millennials who ignore and will not communicate because they don't feel like it or simply don't know how to say no.

Normally Dina and I wouldn't spend so much time on a potential client that is this difficult, but it didn't make any sense. We also knew that the casino was possibly good money and long-term contracts. We continued to set boundaries around the communication we were able to control. Dina suggested going through the backdoor using his company's switchboard to avoid showing our name on the phone when it rang through to the client's office. It worked, and the potential client picked up. He sounded confused and surprised that I got through to his direct line. In his busy state, he offered one gig, not the many he bragged about when we met in person. I booked the date through his team, who handled me exactly like their boss had done, with little to no communication. Dina's experience teaching and working with millennials helped us to break through the unresponsive communication to get a gig booked.

I decided to put my college Business/IT Division Chair hat on to do a better job at reaching our millennial buyer. As Division Chair, I have had the privilege of overseeing a diverse group of technology and business professors that range from Baby Boomers to Gen-Xers to millennials. While millennials get impatient with the Baby Boomer's lack of technology savvy, Baby Boomers get irritated with their lack of interpersonal skills and entitlement. Gen-Xers are stuck in the middle. What I have found in this disconnect is the opportunity to teach one another. I often reach out to my millennial colleagues to walk me through new technology. When appropriate, I try to exhibit and share the etiquette of communication and the value of communication protocols and processes. Good, two-way communication can support new and innovative ideas and activity through reciprocal interactions. In this case, persistence and commandeering communication through the back door may help to temporarily break the barrier with our millennial buyer.

Being responsive and clear in our virtual communications creates confidence and respect with clients. With the advent of social media and texting, we also look for ways to communicate *based on the needs of our end user*. Today that might include sending a text or instant messaging. Responsiveness is still considered good manners and a great way to start a relationship of trust with distribution channel members and the client.

One of our favorite client emails from the Cultural Affair's Officer in Yerevan, Armenia, describes her satisfaction with our quick email responses. "You've been an absolute pleasure to work with -you've been so quick, responsive, clear, and flexible. I greatly appreciate this!" **Tressa Rae Finerty**, *Cultural Affairs Officer -U.S. Embassy Yerevan*[iii]

This is a call-out to all the wonderful and talented millennials who are moving into positions of power in business. You are the future. You must learn to work across a multi-generational workforce and supply chains that require various communication modalities, including face-to-face, telephone, and email based on your end user's communication needs, not solely upon your communication needs. Learn now that in business, the ones who connect are the ones who win.

Not understanding the impact of technology on business communication is dangerous to the bottom line because it completely ignores the new dimensions in which organizations must compete. Leaders, managers, and business owners that are most responsive will have a greater chance of succeeding because they will be able to develop competitive advantages with lower costs and unique value.

Virtual alliance leadership requires multiple roles to build trust for successful outcomes. Leaders must be consistent in their communication and behavior.

Building trust is the key to get beyond cultural differences, increase flexibility, and reduce controls that slow down processes. Responsive, two-way communication can support innovation and strong relationships across workplaces with multigenerational teams. Persistence, patience, and innovative communication help to bridge the generational communication gap based upon platforms of respect.

Hardcore Tips
Chapter 7: Increasing Performance in Virtual Environments

1. Good leadership in virtual environments considers timing, communication barriers, and cultural differences and builds trust before setting out to manage a task for successful outcomes.
2. Leading in a virtual environment across cultures requires communication consistency and accessibility.
3. Decide on negotiation procedures and protocols and promote virtual alliance cooperation through the development of a set of shared values.
4. Effective two-way communication can support performance within multigenerational teams by selecting an appropriate communication tool based on the end user's needs.
5. Responsive and clear communication sets the parameters for positive channel member relationships that benefit the client.

#deospeaks

CHAPTER 8

Create Platforms of Respect

W alking through the open-air courtyard of the Turkish restaurant, the aroma of flatbread baking in the outdoor brick oven enticed me right through to the ornate wooden doors. The smell of the fresh, crisp bread made my mouth water for the delicious steak kabobs, tomatoes, onions, and cool cucumber dill sauce that was sure to come my way. Ahmet, one of the many hard-working MWR Directors I had the pleasure to work with, gave me a sidelong glance when we entered the restaurant lobby. With a twinkle in his eye, I knew what Ahmet was suggesting. I guided the newest band member to the front to cue the waiter as to who would be the target of the toothpick cut sock prank. Ahmet took care of the rest of the prank set up when he excused himself and "went to the restroom."

Every new band member who arrives with us in Turkey at Incirlik Air Base had to pass our MWR

Tour Director's restaurant initiation. The initiation always starts the same way. The band arrives at the designated restaurant. To get service, the new person must take off their sock and shoe, placing their bare foot in a bowl of warm water, while cutting a toothpick in half on a wooden plank with a machete. The waiters demonstrate the technique as a custom of the region. The cleaner the cut, the better the skill of the swordsman. If the band member buys into the fun (who doesn't want to cut a toothpick in half with a machete?), the waiter brings out the hidden element of the prank. The best swordsmen in the region use a blindfold with one foot in a bowl of water while cutting the toothpick clean.

Blindfolded and guiding their hands, the waiter instructs the new band member to cut in half what they think is a toothpick. Swapping out the toothpick for the removed sock once the blindfold is in place, and their foot is in a warm bowl of water, the band member unknowingly cuts through their own sock. Quickly replacing the sock with a cleanly cut toothpick before the blindfold is removed, the whole restaurant applauds. It isn't until the band member puts their sock back on that they realize they just cut their sock in two. As a medal of honor, and through all the laughter, the waiter then tacks the cut sock to the restaurant wall with the name of each player.

Dina Preston Band Sock Initiation in Adana, Turkey, 2004

Don and I had a good relationship with Ahmet, so during our 3rd tour when we arrived a day late, a bit battered from 40 hours of travel and a difficult customs' entry the last thing we wanted to do was perform that evening. We were toast.

Our entertainment contracts always state that if we travel more than nine hours in a day, we do not have to give a performance the same day. It's essential for the band to rest after a long flight or travel day because fatigue affects our physical bodies and ultimately our vocal and musician skills. Like an athlete we are not as sharp when we are tired. Because of the challenges of flying overseas, we sometimes arrive later than expected with a performance schedule within hours of landing.

Don and I pulled Ahmet aside to remind him of our nine-hour contract clause. "I understand," he said, "but we have a change of command and personnel tomorrow. Most of the men and women stationed here are flying back to the U.S., and new personnel is flying-in. It's going to be a while before things get settled on base. If you don't perform tonight, you won't have an audience tomorrow, and then you leave for Italy. It's now or never," Ahmet said expectantly.

Dina and I wanted to help the MWR Tour Director and meet the needs of our service men and women, but we also had a responsibility to our band members to ensure their health and well-being at the start of the tour. We spoke with the band members who said they would perform, but we all agreed to delay the start time, get something to eat, shower and at least rest for a few hours. That did the trick. We performed to a full house of partying airmen and women celebrating the end of their tour of duty and going home. Along with a segment of Karaoke with the band, we were able to draw on their energy and give a solid performance. In celebration of our cooperation and packed show outcome, the MWR Tour Director took us to our favorite restaurant the next day for lunch. Right on cue, our newest band member lost his sock.

Respect is the ability to honor another. Whether it is a colleague who has a different opinion or a client whose idea does not seem feasible, creating a platform of respect is essential for successful performance outcomes. A lack of respect in dynamic environments is counterproductive to success. It breaks the bonds of trust required to move and address issues or opportunities quickly, reduces employee satisfaction and erodes overall morale and team playing.

To support a platform of respect, it is crucial to cooperate as part of the overall value chain to deliver positive results to the client. With a willingness to place individual needs aside for collective goals, cooperation becomes an essential element in creating trust with partners. Cooperation requires collaboration and working things out to the benefit of both parties. By focusing on the result, members of an alliance can better share both tangible and intangible resources that also continue to build the relationship based on trust. Active listening helps with this process.

Dina Preston Band, Outside U.S. Incirlik Air Force Base Entrance, 2004

Active Listening

With eyes wide open and walking briskly towards me from stage left, the medic tried to whisper in my ear, oblivious to the audience below. "What?" I said, turning my head while trying to finger a fast pattern of guitar chords and sing harmony in my vocal mic with Dina. "What is your blood type?" the medic yelled out over the music, oblivious to my struggle to hear him and perform. Narrowing my eyes, I shrugged my shoulder to indicate that I didn't know and nodded at him to go away and get off the stage. With disappointment in his eyes, he calmly ignored my plea and went to each band member performing on stage to ask the same question.

Once the sun goes down, Diyarbakir Turkey becomes a hazardous place for foreigners. Within the beauty of its medieval and Roman walls, and enormous stork nests dotting the telephone poles and chimney rooftops across the city's landscape, you can feel the city's rich history of antiquity as soon as you land.[iv] During the day in the historic cobblestone city streets, children rush foreigners to sell their prayer beads and homemade pretzels stacked on silver trays that they effortlessly balance on their heads. But by the afternoon, the children leave, shops close and the streets become barren to set the stage for what is to come; the good, the bad, and the ugly. In those days the curfew for the air base, home to a small staff of U.S. military personnel and contractors, who guard and work on U.S. intelligence systems, was set at 3pm. Many of the stores were off limits because of possible terrorist activities, as the Kurdish people, a large minority group, have been fighting for independence from the Turkish government for years.

I later learned that one of the base contractors decided to break the curfew to visit a local brothel and was caught in a crossfire attack with a severe bullet wound to his gut. With a rare blood type, the medic who came up on stage was simply trying to save the contractor's life. The contractor was put on our plane and sent to Germany that night. That meant a few extra days in Diyarbakir until a new transport could be arranged for the band. Having issued an apology to the medic for not being more understanding about the disturbance during our show, the band settled in for the next few days waiting for a new transport to be assigned.

After we got our performance assignments for the extended stay, Dina decided to take a nap before the next evening show. I was restless, so I went with the drummer to the outside carpet and jewelry shops. I learned that Turkey is home to a type of woven gold bracelets that you can't get anywhere else in the world. Beautifully handcrafted, the techniques for making these byzantine bracelets have been passed down for two centuries. Priced by the weight, the 18-24 karat gold jewelry in Turkey is also better quality than the standard 14 karat gold found in the U.S. markets. I decided to surprise Dina with one of these beautiful gold bracelets. The shop keeper asked why we were in Diyarbakir. I shared the information on our band's evening performances, and he was very impressed, asking for a signed CD and poster. I communicated that I liked his shop and was interested in one of his byzantine bracelets for my wife.

Haggling is part of the marketplace etiquette. I knew the international price of gold as I had watched Dina haggle in the Incirlik gold shops a few days before. His first price of $120 was a starting point. Somehow between haggling and paying him what I thought was a final price of $75 for the bracelet with a signed poster and CD of the band for goodwill, I, apparently, had gotten the transaction wrong.

Later, grabbing the ringing phone, I stared at the peeling paint on the wall as I listened to the commander's request. "Sure, I can come down. Where are you located? I had been called to the commander's office. The shopkeeper, along with his boss, was now at the military base gates demanding more money. Great, an international incident and we'd been in town less than 24 hours.

Come in, the commander said in a friendly voice. The small green office was sterile and stark, nothing glamorous. The old fan circulated the stale air in the room. Pointing his finger at me, the once friendly shopkeeper, now accusatory, said loudly, "He promised me CD deck." "What?" I said, "I don't even have a CD deck."

In the shopkeeper's version of the story, I had promised $75 and a CD stereo deck, which didn't make sense since I didn't have access to a CD stereo deck and would not have traveled with one. I handed my receipt for $75 that was also marked with plus CD (not a CD player) to the commander who then handed it to the shopkeeper's boss. Confused and embarrassed, the shopkeeper's boss looked at the receipt with a clenched jaw. Shouting, and baring his teeth, he jumped up as his hand came down like thunder on the back of the shopkeeper's head. "Holy shit," we all gasped at the intensity of the moment.

I offered to give back the bracelet knowing Dina wouldn't mind, but they didn't seem to want to part with the $75. The commander was patient and respectful with these community business members. Walking us through the problem by listening and repeating their complaints, he then made a few counter suggestions that fit within their needs. We ended up agreeing to twenty-five more dollars, which I paid.

The store owner left happy. I thanked the commander and apologized for the misunderstanding. The commander shared that this sometimes happened with the local store owners. The key for him was to keep the relationship with the community positive.

Haggling requires the ability to listen well and understand what the other person is saying. The goal of the buyer and seller is to determine a value that is agreeable to both sides. By rephrasing what is being agreed upon more than once and evaluating the situation from both the buyer and seller's point of view, a good deal can be had by both parties. Finding shared value starts with the ability to listen well. The benefits of finding shared values support relationship building.

A Cup of Chai: Building Trust

"Hello, my friends, please come in," in his ankle-length white robe with long sleeves, that fit much like a kaftan, the grey-bearded rug merchant was waving us into his store. His friendliness and wide smile, along with the aroma of frankincense drifting out of the front door, enticed us into his shop.

Taking a seat on traditional oriental floor pillows, I was starting to calculate the amount of money it might take to purchase one of these rugs. The everyday multicolored wool tribal rugs of brown, gold and orange littered the floor or were rolled up leaning against the walls. In each corner of the room, household utility carpets and prayer rugs of red, black and white were stacked to the ceiling. Don and I gazed up at the more expensive baby blue and white ornate silk rugs hanging down like precious tapestry. The silk is so fine in these rugs that children are often the only ones that can see through the sheen clearly enough to knot them. We were obviously in a room full of handmade art.

"Would you like a cup of chai tea?" Yes, we nodded to the merchant. "With sugar, mint or lemon?" he asked. We planned to buy, so we accepted the invitation to enjoy this ritual. We exchanged pleasantries about the weather, the family business, and in our case, made an inquiry about the merchant's favorite type of music. Sitting down on the floor for tea with sugar or mint immediately removed barriers by letting us become friendly to build trust.

"Look, my friends," said the merchant as his sons started to lay out a collection of carpets, "this is wool, this is a mix-medium, and this is pure silk, the best quality."

I was bored. Instead, my eyes went back to the elaborate baby blue and white pure silk sheen tapestry accented with gold hanging on the opposite wall. Right then I decided nothing else would do. Still, I looked away. I didn't want to give him the upper hand in negotiations.

"How much for the red and black wool and cotton blend?" I asked nonchalantly. "Three-hundred dollars," he continued "this is a tribal rug, hand knotted, very hard to find on this street." I shrugged honestly, "I don't like it enough to spend three hundred dollars."

This went on for a while as he kept rolling out carpets for our inspection and I kept shaking my head, no. "What are you looking for madam?" he said, getting a bit exasperated as the carpets started to pile up on the floor in front of me.

"I don't know," I said, holding my ground. "What about that blue and white carpet?" I asked innocently, pointing to the masterpiece.

"Ah, I see you have an eye for quality." "I just like the color," I countered.

"That rug is fourteen hundred euros, madam."

"What is your best price?" I asked as another round of chai tea with mint came out on a tray.

"Twelve hundred euros, madam, this is the finest carpet in the store with many, many knots."

I wasn't in a hurry, so I kept stalling, interjecting small talk about local music, food, and family while sipping tea between haggling. With opposing goals of getting the highest versus the lowest price, we needed to find the middle ground. Bundling the purchase of the red and black wool and cotton blend together with some utility carpets, allowed us to walk out of the store with my beautiful baby blue silk rug at a price that pleased all parties.

One of our favorite pastimes, when we travel in the Middle East, is buying rugs. We love the stunning Persian carpets and tapestries we have collected ranging from Oman to Uzbekistan. Buying rugs in the Middle East has taught us how to build relationships in a short time through simple courtesies.

The tea ritual takes the edge off the haggling experience by taking a moment to find common experiences between the buyer and seller. Sharing common experiences creates bonds on which we can build value that supports both the seller and buyer's needs. Being authentic through shared experiences also allows us to show humility that builds trust.

Don Ortiz and Dina Preston @ Incirlik, Turkey Rug Shop

Humility: Foundation for Progress

"Don, we were asked not to wear our tour shirts. It's not a good idea," I warned.

"I don't have any clean shirts left," Don said as he pulled off his smelly garment. We hadn't been able to wash any clothes since we started the tour, so I empathized. We were all carrying suitcases full of dirty laundry. "Honestly, the logo is not very big, no one is going to notice," Don claimed as he put on the taboo shirt.

When we receive an offer to tour, we also create polo shirts with the band logo and U.S. Embassy country hostname. When it is hot, and we perform outside, the polo shirts look professional and can be substituted for our heavy western wool shirts. They are also great for international travel and media interviews because the polo shirts promote the band's brand with the embassy, helping to identify us and our work when we are in a new country.

Arriving in Armenia, we proudly wore our Armenia and Azerbaijan U.S. Embassy polo shirts. Immediately the embassy personnel said to cover the Azerbaijan embroidery. While we had read that there was some conflict between the two countries, we didn't realize the extent. Armenia and Azerbaijan have no diplomatic relations because of the ongoing Nagorno-Karabakh conflict. Both former Soviet countries, a diplomatic relationship is non-existent as they technically remain at war.

The Armenia embassy personnel warned the band that any garment appearing to promote Azerbaijan would be problematic in their country, especially with the photo ops and television interviews that were lined up. At the same time, we could not be seen promoting Armenia in Azerbaijan. We did what the embassy asked and put our tour shirts away. However, when the band transferred over to Azerbaijan from Armenia through the country of Georgia to continue the two-country tour, Don decided to be a nonconformist.

The odor of fresh paint and construction hit us as we arrived at the newly built seaside resort in Azerbaijan. You could smell the saltwater of the Caspian Sea in the air as we unloaded our gear from the van. Children were screaming with laughter and splashing in the water of the hotel aqua park. Innocently, Don headed down to the pool area to grab a couple of bottles of water for our room. Looking up from his register, the uniformed cashier in his crisp white shirt and white pants, scooping out ice cream as a side gig, started pointing at Don's shirt yelling "Armenia, Armenia" as if to alert others in the store. Like a call to arms, the shouts of Armenia rallied a circle of angry men with clench fists, who, when they saw Don's shirt began to erupt like volcanos. Indignant that anyone would have the nerve to parade a shirt emblazoned with the word Armenia across the front, the livid men continued to shout "Armenia, Armenia" as they closed in on Don.

Slowly backing up, while pointing to the band's guitar and embassy logo to explain his identity, Don quickly looked for an escape route. Heart racing, but keeping his wits about him, Don turned to head back to the safety of our room through the winding corridors of the multi-level hotel. With the mad mob at his heels and trailing behind him, Don circled around the back way to our room through the employee stairs, managing to lose the fuming troop of men.

Rushing into our room, he quickly locked the door behind him. "What's wrong?" I asked. He looked like a ghost. Breathing heavily from running up numerous flights of stairs, Don didn't answer but quickly took off the shirt. I understood and tried not to give him the "I told you so smirk." We still have our Azerbaijan and Armenia tour shirts packed.

Don forgot to consider the deep wounds between the citizens of these two countries over the ease of wearing the only clean shirt he had left. Being humble requires taking out the "me" to support the "we" to better understand and respond to the needs of the client. It also requires situational awareness by respecting the boundaries of others.

Creating an environment of respect starts with the ability to listen and understand what the other person is saying. Active listening supports our ability to develop a platform of respect through cooperation and understanding differing viewpoints. Humility helps us find and act on alternate solutions in difficult situations that might not be your own.

Dina Preston Band with Ambassador Anne Derse,
U.S. Embassy Azerbaijan, 2007
Photos courtesy of Dmitri Tarahovsky

Hardcore Tips

Chapter 8: Create Platforms of Respect

1. Cooperation by placing individual needs aside for collective goals is an essential element in creating trust with partners.
2. Finding shared value starts with the ability to listen well. To ensure complete understanding and build rapport between the seller and buyer, paraphrase key negotiation points.
3. Sharing common experiences creates bonds that support trust and value based on both the seller and the buyer's needs.
4. Humility can increase performance by being willing to admit to mistakes to create a better course of action.

#deospeaks

CHAPTER 9

Order in Chaos

"Hey, I don't want to alarm you," said our military escort as we jumped off the helicopter at our third mountain operations stop, "but the radar has just picked up something trying to lock on our helicopter." The band looked up at him quizzically. "Heat-seeking missiles," he continued. "We need to make this a short meet and greet. It's imperative we get back to base command ASAP." The mountains were full of Serbian warriors with air-to-ground missiles pointed to head straight at any Macedonian target with an element of surprise. In this case, the target was our CH-47 Chinook helicopter and its cargo, us. When close enough, the missiles would turn on their own radar and explode on impact.

Established along the former Yugoslavia border is Camp Able Sentry. As a staging area for NATO military peacekeeping forces in Kosovo, the U.S. had a large military presence when we arrived in the blistering summer of 1998. The objective of the camps was to report activity between the borders of the former

Yugoslavia Republic of Macedonia and Serbia to maintain peace and the region's stability.ᵛ Our mission was to entertain U.S. troops stationed in the area. The region was not always peaceful.

In addition to our scheduled show on base, Dina, and the band were flown in a CH-47 Chinook helicopter to meet, greet and play a few acoustic songs to small groups of special operations forces along the Macedonian and Serbian mountain boarders. We boarded the tandem-rotor chopper and strapped in for the heavy lift ride to the mountain top operations stops. With speeds of up to 196 miles per hour, the takeoff and landing were swift and fast.

Armed with acoustic guitars, fiddle, and a keyboard the band arrived to offer an intimate concert to the Special Operations point men who were rotating on a twenty-day cycle of solitude. While Don and the band played, I often two-stepped with the soldiers, listening to their wishful stories of home.

Dina Preston Band heading to Macedonia Serbian Mountain Opts

It was tense as we all loaded back into the helicopter to take off. As leaders, we kept our focus on the commander and sharpshooter assigned to go with us. They were in constant communication with the home base through their headsets. As we watched for changes in their eyes, the helicopter made an abrupt takeoff. We all leaned hard to the left. This flight was going to be different.

"Hold tight" shouted the Colonel over the noise of the rotors as we started our ascent. Zigzagging, and hugging the ground, the pilots were flying the Chinook up and down using the folds of the terrain as their guide. Skimming the tops of the trees to avoid being a target in the sky and staying under the radar, the pilots were using air-to-ground maneuvers to get us back to camp.

The pilots had no time to think about what had to be done. Going into execution mode, they were well trained to quickly break down their flight plan into small steps. They were agile, nimble, and committed to the maneuver. When the wind picked up, the pilots had to be creative and strategic to make accurate forecasts and avoid critical errors in judgment that might land us in a crash in the fields below.

When we landed at Camp Able Sentry, the commanding officer met us at the landing pad to share that we were in no official danger. The rebel forces had been quickly taken out by the base's air power during our flight back to base.

That night the band celebrated with the camp. Along with a home-made cowboy buck and barrel rodeo competition, complete with a Team Preston win, we played music for them all night. By the end of our impromptu show, the crowd was carrying the band members on their shoulders and singing God Bless America.

Working for government entities like the Department of Defense and the U.S. State Department requires readiness in various types of situations. From performing in military theaters or designated war zones to working across business borders between countries, we are one piece of a much larger system of interconnected parts. While logic reveals that the whole is greater than the sum of its parts, it's important to understand the parts to get the best out of the whole to develop critical thinking skills. The Chinook helicopter pilots did this well in a stressful and perhaps life-threatening situation. Breaking the whole into parts allowed them to expertly execute each task so we might live to perform another day.

In business, breaking the whole into parts supports critical thinking at its best by learning how to evaluate each part and its influence on the larger outcomes. The strength is not in learning how to calculate, but rather how to reason. Breaking down the sum of the parts provides a foundation for higher order thinking.

Dina Preston Band @ Macedonia and Serbian Boarder-Opt#2, 1994

Lost in Afghanistan: Adjusting and Adapting

"MOVE, MOVE, MOVE!" shouted the army man as he climbed into the tail-end of the C-130, opening to unload troops, pallets full of supplies and gear, and our band. We had arrived safely at Afghanistan International Airport in Kabul. Serving as a U.S. military headquarters for the region, a tight formation of armed men surrounded the plane as we de-boarded. Ready to shoot their AK16 from the hip at a moment's notice, their job was to keep snipers at bay and get us safely from the plane and runway into the terminal for inspection.

After the attacks on 9/11, we were asked to tour "the Stans" to support our troops deployed in Desert Storm II. This included Bahrain, Kuwait, and Qatar, followed by Afghanistan, Uzbekistan, and Kyrgyzstan. We flew into

Qatar for a New Year's Eve performance and were placed on a C130 the next morning for Afghanistan.

The logistics for this tour were last minute. In fact, we did not receive our touring documents or DOD passports until we hit the terminal hallways of Dulles Airport in between flights from Phoenix to London. With such a hectic tour start, we were not surprised when we landed in Afghanistan, and no one knew we were coming.

"What do you mean you don't have an escort? Civilians are not allowed in the theater without a military escort." German Shepherds sniffed our carry-on bags as we stood waiting to pass through personnel and cargo inspection. The guards asked to see our military escort who is required for civilians traveling in an active theater. We had no one.

"Heads are gonna fuckin roll," yelled the Kabul base commander, furious that he was now responsible for 4 civilians in an active war zone. Washington didn't have us scheduled for Afghanistan; it was a mistake. Don later learned that the MWR personnel from Qatar should not have put us on a plane to Afghanistan. After our New Year's Eve performance in Qatar, we were supposed to go back to Kuwait, not on to Afghanistan.

Once in the country, there was no easy way to get out because we came in with a fresh platoon. It might be weeks or months before we could leave for Kuwait. The decision was made to find us an escort and put us to work performing in the theater. Embedded with the military, the band sang our way through the Afghanistan, Kyrgyzstan, and Uzbekistan war zones. In addition to performing, we did meet and greets all over the base to support morale, including the Red Cross, which provided humanitarian operations in the area.

The Apaches are "Hot," said the major, "loaded, and ready to be deployed." Treated as VIPs, Dina and I, along with a few band members, took a ground tour of the Apache helicopters at the Bagram base flight line. A presentation from the Command General in the War Room followed.

Dina Preston @ Red Cross in Kandahar, Afghanistan, 2004

Walking slowly into the darkened wood-framed room with a mess of phone and computer cords hanging from the ceilings and tied to the wooden beam columns, we needed to stay out of the way of military personnel bustling with orders and coordinates from all over the theater. Don and I looked up surprised to see the walls built out with multiple decks and all branches of the U.S. military, along with their lawyers, represented. This group could pull up a ship in the middle of the ocean and give you specific data on the location, type of ship, and speed. They could see everything that was going on in the world, although the purpose of the technology was to handle the war's fiercest fighting areas.

Military leadership made continual changes to their war room strategy based on information that was coming in every few minutes. New data required adaption, adjustment and refining. While top-down command is the rule, teams of military personnel actively collaborated with a shared sense of responsibility for the success and implementation of the war room strategy.

In 2007, Bagram airfield was the target of a suicide bomber that killed 23 people.[vi] A reminder that no matter how powerful the U.S. military, the base was still a target for terrorist activities. We experienced this ourselves when an explosion in a nearby minefield went off while we were inside the command center.

"Thank you for all that you do to keep us safe," Don stood up when the presentation was complete, and the band followed, shaking hands to show our gratitude. "Now it's our turn to take care of you," I followed. Nodding, Don invited everyone to our evening show, and we headed back to our assigned military tent, or hooch, as soldiers call them.

Dina Preston Band @ Bagram, Afghanistan Fighter Jet Flight Line 2003

Dina Preston Band @ Bagram, Afghanistan Command Center

Opening the flap of our army tent set up on four by eight sheets of wood, I sleepily took in the sunshine while pulling up my army jacket collar. Thrusting my hands in my pockets, I needed to guard against the icy wind sweeping through my body on that cold afternoon. Still a bit jet-lagged and waiting for sound check, I must have dozed off in the tent I was sharing with the male members of my band.

"Don," I looked back in the dark tent, adjusting my eyes, "I'm going to head to the showers to get refreshed." While I did have access to a female only shower, complete with a curtain and garden hose, there was no room for modesty. Undressing in a small wooden box with a makeshift two-by-four bench, I stepped in a plastic shower pan and pulled the torn and thin-as-paper shower curtain behind me. Turning the garden hose on low, I quickly got in the freezing cold water, soaped up the important places and with goosebumps all over my body, I rinsed, dried and quickly put my warm clothes back on. My hair needed to be washed, but I wasn't about to do that in the freezing cold shower, naked. We were in a war zone, so I adapted. We all did.

At some of the bases, we dined on field rations with Tabasco, quite the treat, the Tabasco that is, until Don met a group of Jordanian minesweepers who were responsible for clearing the minefields daily. At night Don played guitar for them. In return, they shared their delicious food cooked over an open fire pit. Don's ability to make fast friends helped him to find better resources, a tasty home cooked meal, which he shared with the band.

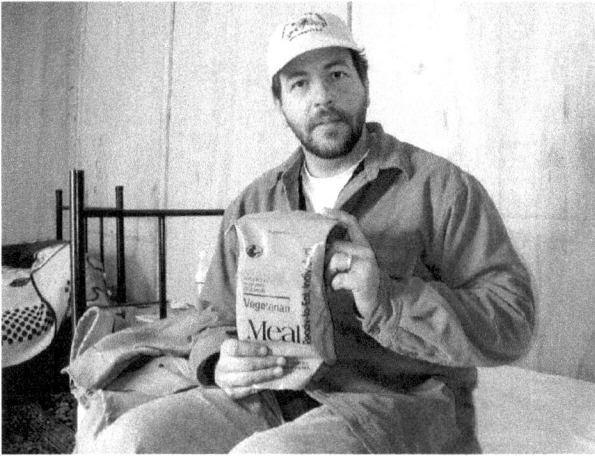

Don Ortiz, Dina Preston Band Afghanistan, 2003

Don Ortiz with Jordanian Minesweepers Kandahar, Afghanistan 2003

Once we made it to Kyrgyzstan our military escort arranged for our first hotel room in weeks. Switching on the light in our lilac smelling guest room, I ran past the white bedspread to the bathroom. Obsessing about the warm, soothing bath I was about to take and the ability to wash the weeks of fine Afghanistan dirt out of my hair, I turned on the tub nozzles to check for hot water. After the quick kiss of happiness I planted on his cheek, Don went down to have a beer and listen to the local jazz trio in the hotel lobby that afternoon. I joined him later for a delicious hot meal of steak and roasted potatoes. It was heaven.

Tucking in for the night, Dina and I quickly fell asleep as the lightest white goose down-filled pillows cradled our heads. After weeks of backbreaking, neck crunching military cots, the Egyptian cotton bed sheets were bliss, providing the ultimate retreat.

It didn't last long. As soon as we started to nod off to sleep, the phone rang. "Don," it was our military escort. "A transport to get you guys out of the theater is leaving in 1 hour. We are 45 minutes away from the runway. There isn't a transport scheduled to go out for another week. Throw everything in your suitcases; we have to go now." The band had just washed their clothes, which were now hanging in our hotel showers dripping wet. It didn't matter, startled from the first moments of a deep sleep, we scooped up our wet clothes, threw them in our suitcases and were off to catch the transport that was leaving in 1 hour.

I must give credit to the musicians who kept a positive attitude at every twist and turn of this trip. Keeping our eye on the objective of entertaining and bringing music from home helped all of us overcome every situation thrown at us. Tour veterans by then, we all knew we had a job to do no matter the conditions, and we did it, no complaints.

Like the shifting conditions of the Afghan theater, risk and uncertainty are everywhere in business. In dynamic structures, adapting to the changing needs of the customer and suppliers is necessary for building a successful competitive advantage. In business, failure is not a result of change, but of the inability of leaders to adapt and take advantage of change and to find new perspectives.

Dina Preston Band, Military Headquarters Kandahar, Afghanistan 2003

Saudi Arabia: Finding New Perspectives

"Okay, Bob, I'm in my office now and will get the paperwork back to you quickly." I hung up the phone and stared at the fax machine waiting for the Department of Defense Saudi Arabia tour documents to generate. The special ring tone followed by a sound like a hundred fingernails scraping across a blackboard meant our paperwork was coming through.

What's this? I wondered as the document was decoded through the phone lines and reproduced on our end. The word DEATH, written in caps, was staring at me from the middle of the page. On closer inspection, Dina and I noticed the document was written in Arabic and translated into English with a seal from the Royal Embassy of Saudi Arabia in Washington, D.C. (See Appendix B, p.159)

I immediately called the Pentagon back, "Bob, I just got the fax. What's up with the DEATH document? Does it really give the Saudi government the right to put us to death? In English, it states that "...any type of illegal drugs and narcotics smuggled in and distributed inside the Kingdom of Saudi Arabia is punishable by DEATH..."

"Don," Bob interrupted my ramble, "If you're going on this tour, everyone in the band has to sign this document, even Dina. It's mandatory. No one working for the DoD gets in without signing this paper. It's part of the contract we have with the Saudi government. Are you in or not?"

During our flight's final descent into Saudi Arabia, Don and I noticed many of the women dressed in western clothing were taking out full-length abayas or black outer garments and head coverings from their carry-on bags. Women up and down the aisles, row after row, were hurriedly covering their bodies head to toe. Putting on the traditional niqab black veil, many women I had just been looking at became faceless. The few American military personnel on board with us were also changing from fatigues into civilian wear. With butterflies in my stomach, I realized I wasn't prepared. Though dressed modestly, I had no abaya or head covering. Lips locked and fanning myself with our military orders, I finally heard the click of the airplane's door being released. I slowly proceeded to immigration and customs with Don and the band in tow. I just needed to do my job, I reasoned, and everything would be okay.

"Who is in charge?" the stern and thin as a rod customs official with the five o'clock shadow asked as Dina tried to hand him our travel orders. "I am," Dina said politely. Dina was used to leading the band through the travel logistics, so it was a natural response. He ignored her and the paperwork. Agitated, he said again, "WHO is the manager?" Once more, Dina said, "I am."

In his khaki uniform and a black beret with the gold Kingdom seal, the officer was visibly irritated, but Dina, though polite, wasn't backing down. Reading the custom officer's body language, I sensed danger and stepped in front of Dina to take over. The officer quickly took the papers from Don. Once through customs, our mili tary escort met us on the other side with an abaya in hand for me. I promptly put on the plain rayon caftan and black headscarf. With only my hands and red nail polish peeking out from behind the long black sleeves, my gender and social status in this country were then clearly defined.

Looking out of the black-tinted windows of our SUV, I took in Riyadh's landscape. With a combination of ancient mud and straw walls hiding the old quarter and modern mosques sounding the call to public prayers five times daily, the city was a juxtaposition of old and new. The open-air souks scattered among various marketplaces were brimming with women walking in full black garb, making them look more like black moving objects than individual people. These women strollers, usually in pairs, were full of energy. As they walked along in the open-air markets, they stopped to admire the ornate gold jewelry hanging in shop windows, or to smell spices spilling out of burlap bags stacked on the walkways.

As we drove to Prince Sultan Air Base, I learned the rules for women in this conservative Islamic country. Outside of Prince Sultan Airbase, I walked three steps behind Don wholly covered in my abaya. Outside the base, public places were segregated by gender, except for the souks where I could enter with Don or another female.

In the 120-degree melting Arabian heat, intensified by the concrete sidewalk and my stifling black garment, water poured out from my skin as fast as I drank it. From one hand to the next, but not saying a word, the attendant in his stained smock passed me my food order through a Ladies Only window. With my head throbbing and feeling tired, I sank my teeth into a rich marinated mix of lamb and beef stacked inside a warm flatbread with tahini yogurt sauce. Trying not to pass out from the heat and feeling a bit nauseated, I thought this is what it must feel like to be segregated, but not equal.

I was not allowed to speak to or be in the company of my male band members, who were inside the air-conditioned restaurant enjoying their meal. There was to be no physical contact with anyone. Don and I didn't hold hands, kiss, or embrace in public. On the streets of Riyadh, I walked behind Don covered and quiet.

From a purely western woman's perspective, the abaya hid my identity in public places, while singling me out as female. I always thought that if the purpose of the abaya was to draw attention away from being a female, it did the opposite. On the street, you cannot help but notice the hundreds of black moving bodies. On the other hand, unless someone got close to me, they did not know I was foreign, so I received many of the same courtesies as local women, kind and courteous hospitality. While the conditions I was experiencing as a female were far different from home, I decided to remove my judgment and change my perspective. Covering was the law of the land. Not covering meant being arrested by the mutawa who enforce Sharia laws such as gender segregation and daily prayer observance.

Working in Saudi Arabia, a conservative country, especially for women, was a great lesson in learning to be open-minded. From signing a death document to covering with an abaya, as a western woman, I learned cross-cultural skills such as tolerance for uncertainty, and empathy that only comes from walking in another's shoes. Being open-minded is helpful when moving through ever-changing environments.

Having an open mind may include giving up control or realizing that you have no control. Lack of control may make a person vulnerable, but it's that vulnerability that widens your world with options you may not have considered. We went back to Saudi Arabia many times after our first visit, considering it a privilege to be one of the few female western singers to experience its rich culture and heritage.

Dina Preston in Riyad, Saudi Arabia @Women's Only Window 1999

Hardcore Tips
Chapter 9: Order in Chaos

1. Breaking down the whole into parts provides a foundation for higher order thinking and strategy development.
2. In dynamic structures, adapting to the changing needs of stakeholders is necessary for building a successful competitive advantage.
3. Failure is not a result of change, but the inability of leaders to take advantage of change to find new perspectives.
4. Being openminded supports learning cross-cultural skills and acceptance for uncertainty.

#deospeaks

CHAPTER 10

Problem Solving

We flew into Charles De Gaulle Airport on December 23, 2001, on our way to perform for those serving in the Mediterranean for *Operation Enduring Freedom*. Rivaling Heathrow in terms of sheer size and never-ending airport terminals, passengers are always in a hurry to get to their next connecting flight. Keeping their heads down, travelers quickly move and shuttle through the terminal walkways with silent efficiency. This time as we left our plane, Charles De Gaulle Airport looked different.

The 9/11 attacks made our flights more complicated and, in some cases, uneasy. The airlines struck in 9/11 included United and American Airlines. We used these commercial airlines all the time to get to our overseas locations. Our passports belonged to the Department of Defense, so we would easily be identified as Americans working for the government in case of an emergency, which might be good or bad given the terrorists roaming Europe.

Searching for information, we found what we were looking for emblazoned on the television screens scattered throughout the airport. Everywhere we turned, our eyes met with CNN 's "Breaking News" red banners with images of a thin six-foot four-inch man with sunken vacant eyes and coarse black hair tied in a ponytail in an orange jumpsuit, handcuffed and being taken into custody by authorities. We hadn't heard about the Shoe Bomber attack until we arrived because we were flying into Charles De Gaulle, as the British terrorist was flying out, with a plan to detonate his shoes filled with explosives and take down the plane.

Richard Reed left Charles De Gaulle Airport on December 22 on American Airlines Flight 63 to Miami. During the flight he attempted to blow up the plane using explosive devices in his shoes. Trained in Afghanistan by al-Qaeda, his attack was thwarted by passengers on the flight.[vii]

Don and I were not aware of al-Qaeda's training camps yet because our trip to Kandahar, Afghanistan, would not take place for another year. Still, it gave us a chill to think this man was a part of the global jihad network continuing to take innocent lives. We quietly wondered if there were more Richard Reeds roaming around the airport and if our flight was next?

Stopping only as part of a layover, the band boarded our next flight out of Charles De Gaulle to Istanbul onboard Turkish Airlines. Still feeling uneasy, by luck Don and I secured good seats towards the front of our Airbus as we boarded. The weather was poor, with heavy sheets of rain and low clouds. Bobbing in our seats, the takeoff was a bit rough. Still, we settled in once we hit cruising speed.

Nestling into Don's shoulder, I took a deep breath and was about to take a nap after a tension-filled morning when I heard a loud "KA-BOOOOM"!! The right side of the plane rocked and dipped. The aircraft continued to shake as the pilots rebalanced the wings. Along with all the other screaming passengers on the plane, I knew we were going to die.

I immediately looked over at Don. He turned his head from the window, squeezed my hand and calmly said: "it's lightning". Our plane had been struck by lightning, a direct hit to the right wing. The skin of the aircraft absorbed the lightning with no real issue to the flight. The pilots stabilized the plane, and the flight continued.

Flying post 9/11 had not become the new normal yet, so I admit I was scared. Experiencing the shaking and boom on the airplane after leaving the same airport as the shoe bomber was disconcerting. The whole plane went from talking and laughter to dead silence for the remainder of the flight. I had a hard time focusing on anything but my fear. I snapped at anyone who tried to start a conversation with me during the rest of the flight. I just wanted to get off the plane, NOW. Don was smart enough to just hold my hand and leave me alone.

Dina was so caught up in the events happening around us that she let her fears get the best of her. By staying calm, I was able to assess the situation quickly.

There wasn't a bomb, lightning and turbulence had hit the plane, and we were still flying. For now, we were okay. In the coming days, Dina and I started to discuss the possibility of how we might handle a terrorist crisis if we were ever to be unlucky.

Making decisions in external environments may involve some doubt because risks can be complicated, uncontrollable, and unforeseen. Managers must watch out for poor problem framing that leads to inadequate or bad decision making and outcomes.

Even though there may be a condition of risk, clearly defining the actual problem and not the symptom of the problem supports better solutions. When a solution just doesn't seem to be working, it may indicate the actual problem has not been identified. Perseverance is important in these situations.

Staying calm and clearing one's mind helps leaders assess and better define the problem. Once the problem is clearly defined, and not just the symptoms of the problem, managers can create and carry out a plan. Discussion on how you can handle a crisis prior to an event also helps to reduce stress levels by being better prepared. We landed in Turkey with no incident, but the experience did change our perception of travel. Staying aware and vigilant without panic was now an essential trait as we continued to move through these uncertain environments.

Muscat, Oman

"Come with me," said the Omani customs official abruptly to Don. Don was escorted down the hall and out of sight of the band, but not before he gave me a quick sideways glance. His hazel eyes, more yellow than brown, told me not to worry. Looking down at the newly waxed floors shining under the fluorescent lights, Don turned the corner and was gone.

When we arrived in Muscat, Oman, a small country on the coast of the Arabian Peninsula, we expected a smooth entry through customs. By this time, we had customs' processing down pat, including checking which countries needed a carnet and which didn't. Much to our surprise, we were detained at customs and inspected.

"I'm sorry," said Don, "I am not allowed to leave my equipment behind or in storage for any reason. It goes where I go. Those are my orders. Is something wrong?" "The paperwork is not in order," said the Omani customs agent as he waved the carnet in Don's face.

"That's impossible, the carnet was stamped and approved by U.S. customs agents before we left," Don suggested with a more assertive tone.

I grabbed my tool bag, ready for what was to come next. The customs agent painfully made me unscrew and match up 30 pieces of equipment to the band's serial number's list. Two hours later it was apparent the customs agent was looking for something, a mistake perhaps, or even an extra guitar that we might have stowed away to sell in the country. I knew American music equipment was hard to get in many foreign countries and often brought premium prices. Once the serial number check was complete, the customs official and what looked to be a local police officer took me.

Sandwiched between the two officials, I was escorted to a storage room filled with what looked like contraband items from antiquity. There were also wooden shelves, built into the walls, towering to the ceilings and filled with every type of highend liquor you can imagine. There were also empty bottles of Courvoisier XO and my favorite, Macallan's rare casks single malt in the corner of the floor. At least the agent and officer appreciated a good drink I thought. "This is the storage room where we'll house your confiscated equipment until further notice," remarked the police dryly. Repeating myself, I said, again, "I'm sorry, but I'm under orders not to leave my equipment behind for any reason. It goes where I go. Those are my orders. We'll have to stay put until we figure this out."

Next stop, the back office with piles of papers, documents, and stale air. We sat down, and they started asking me the same questions again--why were we there, where were we going, how were we getting to our destination in Oman and when were we leaving the country. I repeated my answers. I tried to be gracious, and though I was tired from traveling, I told the truth and stuck to the documents.

Into our third hour, I took a risk and innocently asked the customs official about the empty liquor bottles I saw piled in the storage room. I politely inquired whether the country of Oman allowed alcohol like Bahrain? I don't know why, but that question immediately stopped the interrogation.

He quickly stood up and walked me down the corridor to the band and baggage. The customs official motioned for everyone to get up. We started to organize the gear to walk it out with us. He didn't stop us. We walked behind him, and when he opened the door to the other side, we saw Department of the Defense and U.S. Embassy officials waiting. Four hours into the experience we were all grateful to see support on the other side. I thanked the custom official and gave him an autographed poster. I knew we were coming back to exit the country after our shows and might run into him. I wanted no hard feelings.

Staying aware and present in the moment allows managers to observe and scan for opportunities when there is a need for rapid problem-solving with limited resources. Being polite when working across bureaucracies with a simple thank you or offering small gifts demonstrates thoughtfulness and respect.

Osan, South Korea

"Dina Preston, please come to the ticket counter." We were finishing up our third tour to South Korea at Osan Air Base, waiting for our C130 to arrive and take us to Okinawa. Along with its primary mission as the 51st Fighter Wing combat operations headquarters; Osan Air Base is an entry and exit point for U.S. military personnel and families. It is a large and busy base. We had the morning to shop at the small box stalls located just outside the base gates before heading to our next tour stop.

After picking up the band's new black satin tour jackets with a classic fiery dragon embroidered on the back, Don and I realized we were running late to catch our flight to Okinawa. We just made it to the boarding area in the hanger when my name was announced over the loudspeaker.

I was informed that our gear pallet was being removed for a casket of a colonel who had recently suffered a heart attack. That meant someone had to stay behind with the gear. There was a typhoon coming in, so the plane had to leave immediately. I had to get on the flight as I had all the logistics information for our arrival in Okinawa. Also, I would be unable to load or unload equipment from the pallet if necessary. The band members decided to flip a coin to see who stayed behind, but Don stepped up and volunteered. He thought he would be joining us on the next flight out, perhaps two or three hours behind the band's arrival in Okinawa, so it was no big deal. Boy, was he wrong.

After the band left, I went to eat at a small Mexican restaurant right outside the gate. I was scheduled out on the next flight once the typhoon passed. Dina departed so quickly that we didn't talk about money. We were low on cash anyway as we were going to pick up our pay that day in Okinawa. While I had a credit card for emergencies, I didn't have much money. I had enough for a cheap meal, ten dollars to be exact. Expecting to board the next plane when I returned, the typhoon had been upgraded to a class four and was moving directly over Okinawa. No flights were going out that day. Still, I had to stay close to the airport because I was flying standby with the equipment pallet.

I went to the Morale, Welfare, and Recreation (MWR) office to see if they could help. It was closed. I went to the USO office. The base was hosting war games. No rooms were available anywhere. I walked all day and kept looking with no luck. Towards the end of the day, I decided to take a shower at the gym to wipe off the grime and get a second wind.

There were still no rooms. I couldn't leave the base and didn't have money for a private hotel, so I decided to sit in the lobby of the closest airport billeting office and wait on the couch in the hope that someone might not show or cancel their reservation. The front desk knew my plight because I had been in several times that day to check room availability. At least I could spend the night watching tv in the air-conditioned lobby until my next round of ninety-nine cents buttermilk pancakes.

I must have fallen asleep at some point and felt a tap on my shoulder that made me jerk up. I was afraid that the front desk person was waking me up to tell me to move. I felt like a vagrant. Instead, he said, "I have a bed open for you right behind this building." It was 4:00 am, so he gifted me the room. When I went inside, I saw that it was a shared room with a body already in the other bed. I stripped because my clothes were starting to smell. After being on my feet all day, laying on crisp sheets in the air conditioning was heaven.

I checked the flight the next morning, but it was still not scheduled to leave. The typhoon was moving slowly. I called NORAD to get updates, but there were no flights to be found. I finally got hold of someone at MWR who helped me get another night at the same billeting.

A few hours of delay turned into four days. I was into a daily routine now. Go to the airport first thing in the morning to check flight availability 2) have ninety-nine cent pancakes 3) hang out at the terminal on standby 4) once the flight was canceled, walk the base 6) have a hamburger for dinner and 7) go to bed early.

When I arrived to check the daily transport on day four, I was told they were sending me with the pallet to another base two and a half hours away. I was assigned a driver and a truck. Once they wrenched the pallet up on the truck and locked it down, off we went. I was relieved.

I asked the kid driver if he knew Korea well. He said he just arrived the day before. I asked if he knew the way to our destination. He said no, but he had directions. I asked him how long he had been driving trucks. He said he just got out of training school and this was his first job assignment. Oh boy. I really couldn't miss that flight.

About two hours into the drive, we got off the highway and headed into a rural area. This didn't look right to me. Most bases were in the city or had an infrastructure with a tower or gate. I didn't see any such clues. All I could see on the horizon were fields of rice patties neatly sectioned out into squares. I realized we were driving on the access road of these fields. With only four inches of dirt on each side, the road was made for an ox and a cart, not a doublewide axel truck. Time was ticking, and we were already running late for the plane. The road became a dead-end with no way to turn around.

I open the door and used the running board to climb along the edge of the truck because there was nothing but swampy wet fields at my feet. Since we were unable to turn the truck around, it was up to me to guide the one-mile back-up. The farmers in the wet rice fields started running towards us, yelling and shaking their fist. I waved backed and shouted, "Annyeonghaseyo, mian-hayo, kamsa-hamnida." "Hello, I'm sorry, thank you." I kept navigating for the driver.

Finally, heading in the right direction, we were back on the highway when we spotted a couple of helicopters flying above us. We also noticed an army fuel truck a few cars up. I told the kid to follow the truck. What did we have to lose at this point?

We arrived at the gate a few minutes later to the sounds of the C130 revving up its engine. We got through the gate and to the runway just as they were closing the plane's back rear ramp. We started flashing our truck lights and beeping our horn as we drove down the runway. We must have looked crazy. Miraculously the crew of the C130 heard or saw us and reopened the back ramp. The loadmaster quickly hooked up the C130 wench to the pallet loaded on the back of the truck. With dirty clothes on my back and two dollars left in my pocket, I landed in Okinawa 3 hours later with Dina and our escort waiting for me as I deplaned.

Even the best-planned tours require on the spot problem-solving. Decisionmaking is a challenge because of the complication and the lack of control you often have over the situation. Finding anchors in a world of chaos helps find solutions that work.

When a turn in the road takes an organization left, and they should have gone right, managers can reconstruct the situation one issue at a time to improve problem framing and get the team to the end goal. Being resilient until the right resource presents itself to solve the problem is also crucial in environments you can't control.

Dina Preston Band @ DMZ South Korea 1993, 1996, 2000 & 2008

Hardcore Tips:
Chapter 10: Problem Solving

1. Clearly defining the actual problem and not the symptom of the problem supports better solutions and outcomes.
2. Manage a possible crisis by developing contingency plans to ease stress and empower employee action.

3. Be aware and present in the moment to scan for opportunities when there is a need for rapid problem-solving with limited resources.
4. To move your team to the end goal, rebuild one issue at a time to improve problem framing and decision making.
5. Be resilient until the right resources are available.

#deospeaks

CHAPTER 11

Leveraging Your Relationships

With my head thrown back, I stabbed my guitar towards the two steppers who were already complaining to the bartender that I was too rock and roll for country. With my long curly hair, I already looked too loud, even before I hit my first note. Ending the song with a speedy Guns and Roses guitar riff just to piss them off, Dina's cheeks were burning as she glared at me and one of the dancers yelled from the floor "that ain't no country, son." I shrugged, mouthed I was sorry to Dina (I wasn't) and yelled back, "Hey it's Slash meets Bakersfield. It's a new sound." I behaved the rest of the night, settling into more traditional country pickin'.

"Man, you know we're playing country music?" said my bar beaten drummer as Don came out of his room the next morning. Don had only been on the road with my band for a few weeks and his innovative, and sometimes off-putting Frank Zappa music was crushing the honky-tonk sounds of George Strait that Charlie had blaring out of the kitchen's boom box that morning. I just had a headache and hoped Don would come around to see the simple beauty in country music.

Don always approaches country music with an edge. He isn't a chicken pickin kind of player but plays traditional country licks with the fire of Santana and, like Gary Moore, can move through country, rock, blues, funk, R&B and dinner jazz with ease. I didn't know it at the time, but he was molding us into something much more than a traditional country band.

"Hey, the client wants us to sing ZZ Top and Lynyrd Skinner tonight." No one else in the band had the voice to sing classic rock, so I took on songs like Tush by ZZ "Top and Guns" and Roses' "Sweet Child of Mine." Don was stretching my abilities. At the same time, classic rock taught me to get down and dirty with my voice, and I was having a blast being gritty. We started to get additional work.

Clients coming to Arizona in the Meeting and Events Industry wanted a western theme experience, though most of the participants were from back east or were international. After a few sets of country music, they were more than ready to rock-n-roll. Because of Don's influence, we could easily add dance tunes for the party part of the evening.

Our song list became vast. With about 200+ songs from different genres we could do a whole night of country, eras music (40s-today's hit), classic rock, acoustic or light dinner music, or a night that included a variety of all genres based on the age, demographic, and even the specific need of the event. We were customizing for each event and didn't realize it. We left our set lists behind. They didn't work.

On stage, we performed moment to moment, no song list. Our musicians learned to start songs by listening for musical intros or even eye or hand signals. This ensures no event is ever the same because we tailor it by the minute. It also gives us the flexibility to change music styles if a song is not working. By taking advantage of our different abilities, Don and I, along with the band, can create a musical experience based on the needs of the audience in the moment. To date, we continue to get 5-star reviews with awesome comments like (See Appendix C, p.161)

"Simply put in 3 words, the Dina Preston Band was sensational, dynamic and AWESOME!!!!! A mix of country, pop, rock, and patriotic songs earned them a well-deserved standing ovation." Rabbine H., Bend, Oregon By leveraging our different music perspectives, Don and I were able to extend our music catalog. It added value to the clients by being able to diversify quickly based on the needs of their guests. Music genre diversification has been profitable for us, too, because it gives us a competitive advantage over other entertainment who may be focused on one type of music. Being able to move well through many styles of music based on the needs of our client's gives us pride in what we do. We consider our audiences partners in the art of delivering a distinct music performance with world-class fun.

The Riga Express to Moscow

Quickly sitting up, I jumped out of bed to dress while Dina slept unaware of the screeching wheels on the train tracks coming to an abrupt halt. I cracked the cabin door to see hulk-like Russian border guards in their long brown winter coats with bright red lapels and gold rank crests, climb on board the train along with long shoulder rifles and sidearm holsters unsnapped and ready to use. "Dina, get up," I said quickly closing the door. I waited for the Russian voices yelling across the train's corridor to distance themselves before walking out to see what was up.

We were traveling and performing on behalf of an old and well-respected Phoenix law firm. Our job was to perform as part of a negotiations and culture exchange with a Russian company interested in doing business in Arizona and The United States. In addition to the law firm lawyers, we had two Arizona state councilmen traveling in the entourage.

Don and I settled in our cabin for the long 16-hour winter ride. It was beautiful. A desert girl for most of my life, the long stretches and panoramic views of the wintery and glistening white tundra went on for as far as our eyes could see. With locked hands and snuggling close, Don and I stared steadily out our window, watching the scenery go by like a 3-D National Geographic public broadcast.

At midnight Don and I celebrated my birthday with a glass of Champaign, salmon, and caviar, provided by our Russian hosts, as the train continued to travel through the pitch-black tundra. "I can't believe this," I said to Don dreamily. It was a perfect birthday gift until Don woke me up in the middle of the night.

As soon as I left Dina, I saw border guards through the cracked door of the security detail assigned to us. While we were not special, we were traveling with Arizona State government personnel and our rich Russian hosts. Kidnapping for ransom was not off the table, something we learned from our former KGB guards when we were not allowed to go out and get coffee before leaving Latvia.

From under their bunks, our security detail quickly pulled out a black leather duffle bag. They handed it to one of the border patrol guards, who said something in Russian and turned around and shut the door. I averted my gaze and kept walking the train's corridor to check on our bass player and drummer.

On my way back, the door opened, and out came the border patrol. Keeping my head down, I could see the cash sticking out of the corner pocket of the man who appeared to be the border patrol commander. He was heading directly to our room and Dina. I slowly followed behind.

The border patrol knocked on our door, and I politely motioned from behind that this was my room. To my surprise when we entered, Dina had already pulled our bags out for inspection; she had been alerted by our host that the guards were on the way. The border patrol commander, still with cash peeking out of his top left pocket, simply asked for our passports. They opened them up, quickly stamped them, and were on their way. We watched them exit the train into the snowy abyss. We had just entered Russia.

Moscow was mysterious and beautifully blue-grey as Don and I stepped down from the train in the early morning winter haze. With only 24 hours to see the sites and get ready for our show, it was a whirlwind of events. At nineteen below zero, we had no real clothing to protect us from the weather when we arrived. Our Russian hosts, who greeted us in long mink coats, hats, and gloves of various colors saw our lack of weather protection and immediately took all of us to a fur store where they bought us mink hats to stop our shivering.

After lunch, we headed to one of Moscow's many science centers to set up and sound check for the evening show. With soft yellow walls, gold leaf edging, and grand white columns dotting the landscape of the room, I romantically imagined the antique oil paintings and crystal chandeliers as the leftover remnants of a Russian Romanov royal palace. We rapidly found our marbled performance room.

"Hey, there is no power converter here?" Don lifted his head from his guitar rig as we all went to work checking our equipment. "No power converter, no guitar pedals, no guitar," he propositioned as he looked around for help.

Our tall, blue-eyed interpreter with perfect porcelain skin and light brown hair with golden highlights down to her waist, coolly strutted her white see-through blouse and expensive Russian sable coat over to Don. In a honeyed husky Russian accent, she asked, "What is the problem, Don?" Explaining the need for his guitar pedals, especially as a power trio, she took out her flip phone. Just moments later, our security detail came in out of nowhere with the duffle bag from the train. A second gentleman followed, pulling cash from the duffle bag. Within minutes Don had his transformer. That black leather duffle bag, as soft as lambskin was fast becoming our deliverer and following us everywhere.

That evening, during dinner the musicians from the Bolshoi ballet performed for the negotiating Arizona and Russian entourage. The party moved into our room after dinner. Starting with a traditional Arizona two-step that usually gets legs and feet on the dance floor in time to the swinging snap of the snare drum, someone shouted "play Elvis" as we hit our last note.

"One for the money, two for the show," without missing a beat Don crooned out Blue Suede Shoes. Within minutes the dance floor was packed with free spirits full of vodka. By the end of the evening, the room erupted into a frenzy as the Bolshoi ballet musicians stomped their feet to begin the famous Cossack dance. With hands folded and kicking their legs out from under them, it was the perfect elevation to end a great evening of fun.

After the finale, we rode the elevator up with one of the lawyers, who looked exhausted. It was way past midnight. He commented to no one in particular, "Now they want to negotiate." It made sense. It would give the Russians the upper hand, while still appearing to be most generous hosts, which they were.

Historically Russians have leveraged relationships through informal networks of payment to secure goods and items that might otherwise not be available due to short supply or government red tape.[viii] During the border inspection on the train and while Don was setting up, band business required both economic transactions and social relationships.

The final negotiation didn't happen until the last night, and it was not a straightforward approach. From Riga to Moscow, our clients (and subsequently, the band) were wined and dined, given only the best. Even as the relationships between the two parties developed, the Russians chose to negotiate very late in the trip, which was to their advantage.

As an American business, we cannot legally follow many Russian business practices. However, we did learn the importance of creating personal relationships by moving slowly to develop a bond of friendship and trust through social events. We also learned that social events are part of an informal negotiation tactic that can make or break a deal.

Finding common ground or shared values that both parties can support, helps to balance cultural differences in global business. Negotiations were more than likely always going to take place late in the evening as the Russians had the upper hand as the host. However, the American team may have inquired about the negotiation schedules in advance to better support their own talents. We left Moscow early the next morning.

Dina and Don @ Red Square in Moscow, Russia 2002

Hardcore Tips:
Chapter 11: Leveraging Relationships

1. Leverage organizational talent by merging unique employee skills that support a competitive advantage contributing to growth.
2. Create personal relationships through social events before negotiations begin. However, never lose sight that social events are still a part of the negotiation process. Stay alert and don't let your strategic guard down.
3. In global environments, negotiations may not always be a linear process. Have patience.

#deospeaks

CHAPTER 12

Keep Clients Coming Back for More

Heading to the bar for another round of cowboy coffee, I was glad to be finished with the set. Getting people on the dance floor that night was like crawling up a steep hill on your knees with a ton of rocks on your back. Heading towards the old western bar that reminded me of northern Arizona's historic Whisky Row, a man blocked my way, eager to tell me that "No girl should be singing a man's song" and "I don't like a girl singing that song."

When Don and I decided to settle in Phoenix, we found it tough to compete with the local country male-dominated hat bands. The live music listening public wanted to hear George Strait and Alan Jackson with maybe a song or two from a female artist. None of my band members had a country voice or didn't sing at all. That left most of the singing to me.

I wanted to sing the songs I liked. It was the quality of the song, the singer's talent, but not the gender of the singer that moved me. It never crossed my mind that a song like The Dance by Garth Brooks had a strict code of gender. However, if I sang a song by a male country singer, I'd often get negative comments from the audience during a break.

The Phoenix country music nightclub scene was hard to crack for a band with a female lead. While we found work in the local bars, it was usually during an off night like Thursday or Sunday. We could never seem to get the headliner position in Phoenix, even though we were an award-winning band in California, and we headlined in clubs across the U.S. and abroad in countries like Canada during the famous Calgary Stampede. In the early 1990s, we were barely making a living. Going back on the road full time was not an option with our son now in school.

To help with the bills, Don and I started taking on odd jobs. One night while serving at one of the local resorts for a corporate event, I saw my first corporate band perform. The stage was beautiful, the band looked great, was well taken care of and best of all they were very average in talent. Nothing special. I knew I could easily play this type of venue and do it better.

Standing in the employee corridors among a mass of four-tiered steel pushcarts full of food, I saw the band from stage talking to a woman in a black tailored pinstriped suit. She was a representative of one of the larger entertainment agencies in Scottsdale catering to the Meetings and Events Industry. I found her on my next break.

"Hey, I'm Dina," I reached out to shake her hand "I just moved here from California with my road band. Do you have a business card?" I got right to the point. "Sure," said the friendly middle-aged, plump agent without hesitation. "we are always looking for experienced music groups. Give me a call."

It was the last time I would ever serve food for money again. I set up a meeting and brought in our promotional material including a cassette tape, eight-by-ten photo glossy and a typewritten band biography. The agency booked gigs for us immediately, and the pay was great. For one night we were going to make nearly as much money as a whole week on the road. Above all else, they loved a female fronting the band, especially one with a trademark vocal. Why? In a sea of male singers and musicians, we stood out among their talent roster. It was something different they could sell. Within the year, we were no longer a specialty group but were being hired regularly along with offers from other local agencies. At some point, I started surpassing my male counterparts in this high paying industry. We became so successful that a few bands tried to lure Don into joining their groups in the hopes of creating the same magic we seem to generate as a team. Don always stayed put, he knew the magic we created could not be transferred.

While the event industry is dynamic, we still focus on our distinctive competencies to create growth strategies. We've expanded our services and products using Dina's experience as a college professor to now lecture and speak in the business arena based on our global experiences. We continue to develop our competencies in new ways to help us expand our capabilities and give us an edge over the competition.

Others have tried to copy us, but the combination of skills between the two of us are hard to duplicate. Why? Music is a service, and services are difficult to separate from the person providing the service. Even if other bands use female singers, they still don't have the characteristics of my voice or Don's signature lead playing ability. Together we have a distinctive sound. As a service provider, our personalities, and approach to the physical execution of the music determine whether a client is satisfied or not. How we execute the service gives us our competitive advantage.

Bottom line, playing your own game is essential in creating a superior business position. Leveraging your own strengths creates a distinct competency that provides value to the customer through unique skills and services that are hard to copy.

Going the Extra Mile

Climbing into the back of our truck with the help of his MP handler from Luke Air Force Base, the German Shepard slowly sniffed each piece of our gear. As we stood there, watching, we were hoping the pup wouldn't sit down, indicating a problem and more delay. We'd been through a million of these types of checks in higher risk places than our local air force base, but we never took anything for granted.

We looked up as we heard overhead the Blue Angels' tight, flight diamond formations and skilled maneuver practice runs. Wing to wing, with no room for error in their multi-million-dollar F/A-18 Hornet jets, the Blue Angels VIP show was gearing up to start shortly, but the unexpected gate inspection put the band behind schedule for sound check.

"Yeah, we are here, but got delayed for vehicle inspection," Don said to our production team lead on his cell. "I thought you got that cleared ahead of time," the production manager barked. "We're late, and you guys gotta be up and sound checked in 30 minutes". Don steadily said, "I did," keeping his composure, "but gate guards have the right to stop us at any time. I have a call into my base contact on the DSN line, but in the meantime go ahead and check our mics and monitors." Finally getting through to his base contact, Don handed his cell over to the gate guard. With a final under the vehicle inspection mirror sweep, we were given the okay to enter the base.

To provide additional value, Don offers several pre-event meetings and walkthroughs to coordinate the band's site logistics and stage production with the primary objective of the event. Don meets with several different stakeholder groups to ensure protocols to ensure that event logistics are smooth, and communications on the client's needs are clearly understood. However, we always have to expect the unexpected.

Once we passed inspection, we headed to the VIP hanger stage. The security check had put us way behind schedule. Fortunately, Don had all the preproduction with Luke Air force Base completed and the sound team was finished. The crew was on top of running lines and sound checking the system before we arrived. With our microphone presets already in his soundboard from previous gigs, we plugged in, did a microphone scratch test and were playing with 5 minutes to spare.

Don sees and shares with our clients the whole panoramic picture of the event, before it takes place, from the audience viewpoint to production integration and performance coordination. With Don's thorough understanding of professional stage production, his knowledge always helps us to attract and keep clients by making suggestions or solving problems before, during, and after the event.

Sharing expertise is a great way to create value in business because it is customercentric. Customers love special attention and personalization based on their needs. Sharing your know-how also promotes customer loyalty as clients recognize they can depend on your skill to help them solve their problems.

Dina Preston Band @ Blue Angels Hanger Party, Luke Air Force Base 2018

Client Experience Matters

With a few couples dancing on the floor to "My Girl" by the Temptations, we were right on track with our event schedule. From center stage, we all noticed the commotion by the door and a crowd gathering over a man in the dark blue suit now sprawled on the gold carpet floor. We didn't stop playing. We never stop playing.

The meeting planner came up to the stage and yelled "pick it up" while rotating her finger in a circle, which was strange given the point in the program, but we picked the music up. In minutes, the dance floor was packed with people twerking, dancing and just letting loose. The meeting planner gave us another signal with her hands to keep the dance music going. While the group was dancing and having a blast, in came the paramedics. Quickly they put the fallen man (who we learned later was the hired key-note speaker) on the stretcher and took him to the nearest hospital. He had suffered a mild heart attack at the door. The meeting planner was shaken but grateful that we had stayed steady, kept the focus on the dance floor and worked with her as a team.

We know that client experience matters. From our initial client introduction to the music performance, it is the chain of events that influence what the customer thinks, not just the actual product or service. If the client has a negative experience in any part of the service chain, a good product or service will not make up for their dissatisfaction. Clients are influenced by the whole encounter.

Being accessible to the meeting planner, even in the middle of the show while on stage, helped divert attention away from this serious matter. Enabling the hotel to quickly act by keeping people out of the way, our job was to distract the convention attendees. To do this, we had to stay present and accessible to those working in the emergency. This group is now a regular client. They hire us whenever they come to Arizona. We are their band. They are not an exception. We work hard to keep our client's loyalty.

Providing value by being available and giving clients more than what they expect supports a positive experience, especially when things go wrong. Clients want to be confident that products and services are reliable. Their experience needs to be flawless from start to finish. When challenges do arrive, they need to be solved quickly by being present and listening to the client to implement the best solution. Cooperation and assistance among supply chain members to remove or mitigate problems help to build relationships through appreciation. Client appreciation improves customer loyalty.

Hardcore Tips:
Chapter 12: Keep Clients Coming Back for More

1. Look for unique differences that support distinct competencies.
2. Sharing your company's expertise as it relates to your products and services adds value and promotes customer loyalty.

3. Clients are influenced before, during, and after their purchase experience. Provide value through each stage by being present, aware, and reliable.

#deospeaks

CHAPTER 13

Gratitude and Judgment

"Steam rises from a market in Budapest...
A view of Paris from the Eiffel Tower Deck...
A midnight ride on the Orient Express...
I miss my home town and my bed...
Cause I'm stuck at Heathrow again"
-*I Can't Wait to See You Again*

"I can't find the key, but there is nothing in there to worry about," said the patronizing, walking brand name with her Chanel suit, Gucci purse and Louie Vuitton bag with a padlock. Watching this passenger rudely argue with Heathrow's Airport security as to why she couldn't open her carry-on bag made us sigh. "Here we go," Dina observed correctly. Without hesitation, the security detail looked at his associate and said, "Give me a cutter" and just like that the expensive Louie Vuitton bag was cut at its seam. Like a stuffed pinata every imaginable high price cream, lotion, and cosmetic fell out on the metal table, spilling on to the floor — each over the 10 milliliters allowed in a carry-on bag.

One of the hardest airport hubs to navigate is Heathrow in London, an enormous metal and glass jungle with highly polished floors. We bustle through numerous terminals with the sound of every imaginable language filling our ears both on the ground and on the intercom systems. Heathrow is never quiet with its clacking and clicking of heels, roller bags and trollies beeping their horns to move through the walking dead. Managing tightly scheduled, connecting flights between terminals that seem to be miles apart is stressful. Flights are often delayed or canceled. With over 200,000 passengers being processed daily and terrorist attack concerns, the airport security detail methodically checks thousands of individual carry-on bags every hour. Heathrow security can be painfully slow.

Here's how Dina and I cope with Heathrow. First, we pace ourselves. We also try to have a good sense of humor. Antics like people trying to get a carry-on bag of World War II ammunition or banned goods through this tight security system always makes us smile. *Really?*

Instead of being irritated, we might get creative by pulling out our phones and writing a song about the experience. One of our songs pitched at a Nashville Songwriter Association luncheon, I Can't Wait, actually discusses getting stuck in Heathrow again. We've learned the art of being patient; you can only be agitated if you allow yourself to be agitated.

Dina might tend to her students online via her phone or iPad, or we choose to just be still in the moment. If we get bored or antsy, we might play games like "Famous Dead Singers of the World." We can focus on the chaos and stress, or we can find alternatives. We choose to look for alternatives we enjoy, helping us to find gratitude in the moment.

Focusing on the moment quiets the chaos around you and calms the nerves by bringing clarity. Clarity supports new perspectives and creativity based on the moment, being productive or just slowing down to catch your breath.

For us, every moment is a gift and an opportunity to experience something new. Every inch of life is rich, and we never want to miss a single moment. Even with challenges, we try to rise to the occasion. We always look forward to being stuck in Heathrow again.

Dina Preston Band Stuck in Heathrow Again, 2013

Camp America

With my cheeks turning red, I shyly stepped up when I heard my name. "Dina Preston, we present you with this U.S. flag flown over Naval Station Headquarters this New Year's Day for your outstanding performance and dedication to the men and women serving at the Naval Station at Guantanamo Bay."

On our second trip to Guantanamo Bay Naval station, Don and I were completely caught off guard when the commanding officer of the naval station called me forward at a flag dedication ceremony we were asked to attend. We did not expect to receive such an honor, especially next to Johnny Grant, honorary Mayor of Hollywood and Bob Hope's USO right-hand man for over 50 years.[ix]

Guantanamo Bay houses not only American Sailors and contractors but also their families. With its red land crabs and iguanas roaming everywhere, the island looks and acts like a regular naval base with many of the comforts of a small American town. Among the fast food chains, schools, baseball fields and a chapel catering to more than a single religion, one would never suspect the mission taking place downwind.

Scheduled to perform for the men and women who carry out guard duties at Camp Delta, the detention center housing suspected terrorists captured by the U.S. in areas like Afghanistan and Iraq, we had no idea of what we might encounter. Camp Delta replaced Camp-X Ray, a group of temporary chain-linked outdoor cells now overgrown with weeds and inhabited by banana rats.

"Mr. Grant, how was your tour today?" Don cautiously asked the revealer of all new stars on the Hollywood Walk of Fame. Johnny Grant was given a private tour of Camp Delta earlier in the day, and we were all curious about the notorious holding. We were heading down for a show later and wanted to be prepared and not caught off guard. Mr. Grant did not respond to Don's question, silently reminding us that our primary mission as armed forces entertainers was to boost morale and welfare of the troops and family members at Guantanamo Bay, not pass judgement.

That afternoon we entered Camp America through cactus scrubland, zigzagging through a series of concrete road barriers. The razor-sharp barbed wire looped and circled through the perimeter of the camp. Dark green, wooden guard towers with American flags stood proud against the blue gateway of the Atlantic and the Caribbean Sea. The band members in quiet contemplation knew where we were going and wondered what we might see.

Camp Delta was clean but sparse. "I.D. and orders please." Dina and I could tell that the young navy petty officer first class with the dark circles under his eyes must be nearing the end of his 12-hour shift. Looking exhausted, he checked our I.D.'s and paperwork allowing us entry. We were aware of the media and world controversy surrounding the treatment of some of the more notorious detainees. However, it was clear our service men and women were also showing signs of stress.

That night the band performed to a small but appreciative crowd who were able to relax and get some relief from their daily high-pressure working conditions in the camp. It was not a time to be judgmental or biased about the inner workings of the detainee centers. Being judgmental as leaders would have set a tone for our musicians and may have impeded us from doing our job well, bringing relief through music to those working at Camp Delta.

We are grateful every day, even when things are tough. Being content in the moment doesn't mean we shy away from the negative. It means we manage it differently. Finding the value in what we have, in one another and even in our own strength by being less judgmental helps us improve our performance and, ultimately, the outcome for the client.

Dina Preston Band in Guantanamo Bay 2004, 2005

Don Ortiz with the Honorary Mayor of Hollywood, Johnny Grant,
Guantanamo Bay, 2005

Dina Preston Band performing

@ Camp America Guantanamo Bay 2004, 2005

Hardcore Tips:

Chapter 13: Gratitude and Judgment

1. Don't take yourself or the situation too seriously. Have a good sense of humor to start the appreciation process.
2. Being content in the moment doesn't mean shying away from the negative. It means managing it differently.
3. Judgmental behavior is based on assumptions and can sabotage organizational performance.

#deospeaks

Part Three: Work Verses Life Balance

"There is no such thing as an ordinary life"
-Mark Twain

It's 5 am, and the dark French roast coffee aroma is slowly making its way up two flights of stairs and into the home office Don and I share. I'm starting to salivate as I wait for Don to bring me a cup of his smooth, velvety coffee with fresh cream. I affectionately yell out

"please HURRY with the café con-leche," because I'm moving at a glacial pace. With only a few hours to write before I must be across town in my college office, I desperately need Don's coffee, ideas, and kiss. They are my morning fuel.

We have been blessed to experience extraordinary events in our professional lives, but in truth, Don and I are quite ordinary. It has been our everyday lives as spouses, lovers, parents, caregivers to our aging parents and as members of our work, community, and family that have prepared us to tackle the opportunities that have led us to our exceptional experiences.

While perhaps not as riveting as flying into Afghanistan or speaking and performing on behalf of the U.S. State Department's global embassies, everyday life is the glue that holds Don and me together. Whether you are getting ready to start your own company, getting a promotion or thinking about a job overseas, we know it is the day to day hardships and joy that have best prepared us for our own unique destiny. Like us, anyone can live their best life.

CHAPTER 14

Overcoming Professional and Personal Loss

D on and I have been working the gig economy since before there was a formal gig economy. Short term contracts, freelancing, and the lack of permanent jobs and money mean we can rarely say no to most paying gigs. This is especially true when you're raising a family as musicians. We have missed many important milestones because of work, including weddings, funerals, graduation, anniversary parties and even Christmas with our son.

Living everyday life provides useful lessons in how to overcome adversity in business, as the old proverb states, "When life gets tough, the tough get going."

Pregnant and Fired

That evening, the craggy bar owner called me into his dank smelling office. Counting out the band's pay with his yellow smoke-stained fingers, he looked up curtly. With a cigarette balancing between his lips, he exhaled smoke from his tarred lungs and said sternly, "This bar is no place for a pregnant woman." He counted the band's pay and fired me all in the same breath.

I confirmed my suspicions earlier that day. I was indeed pregnant; at 98 pounds I couldn't keep down food. I told the bar owner and a few band members when I arrived at our house gig that afternoon. The steel guitar player with his lamb chop sideburns and curled up cowboy hat, a temporary side man saw his opportunity and seized the moment. He went to the bar owner on the break and offered his services without me. Though I was fired, he was playing there the following week with my drummer, bass player, and a new front singer. I needed to find another job and fast.

With the smell of bacon and Pine-Sol disinfectant in the air, the faux leather booths and dirty marble floors were a constant reminder of the cheap surroundings. I was hoping to find a waitress job with access to daily cash. "Are you pregnant?" my third manager of the day asked as he looked through the application questions. "Yes," I said honestly. The pregnant question was on every restaurant application I filled out, alerting all hiring managers to my condition.

I also started looking for new music jobs, but this time, I kept my mouth shut. I wasn't showing yet, and there were no formal hiring applications, so I picked up a few one-nighters that paid my new group of musicians just enough to keep the lights on, pay rent and my medical bills, and put food on the table. I hid my pregnancy if I was able. If they didn't ask, I didn't tell.

The tipsy audience was enjoying the band competition and, along with the judges, the power to decide the fate of each band. Under the hot stage lights, I looked the audience straight in the eye and said, "As I'm sure you can tell, I'm going to have my first baby soon." The audience roared with applause and gave me a standing ovation when I shared my excitement of becoming a new mother. Six months pregnant, my new band won the semi-finals for the Marlboro Music Round-Up competition in the southern region of San Diego.

"Do you have any openings," I asked the manager as he handed me the winning paperwork. The band was going to the final state competition. "How about a regular Sunday night," he said? I thanked him for not making my pregnancy an issue. "Why would I? My customers don't care, and neither do I."

As an independent contractor, I was not entitled to job protection under the Pregnancy Discrimination Act.[x] That didn't stop the emotional sting of losing my income as a musician. Once I got over the initial shock of being fired from my house job, I looked for resources to make a new plan. I wasn't afraid to seek out help or guidance.

I had a beautiful baby boy and named him Jay. Within three months of his birth, we were traveling to Nashville so that I could audition by invitation for a Nashville cable television show in the back rooms of the Grand 'Ol Opry. My band picked up another house job when my son turned two and the San Diego New Times nominated us in the country category for Band of the Year. Becoming a mother was a gift. Being a working and traveling mother brought new challenges.

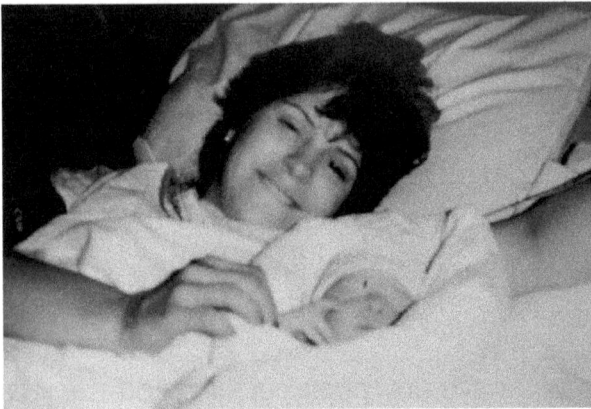

Dina Preston and baby Jay 3 hours old, 1986

Christmas: Leaving our Son

In December of 2001 shortly after 9/11, Don and I received a phone call from John Field, our DOD contact located at the Pentagon. The Pentagon was under repairs from the recent attacks, but the overseas entertainment program was still going strong. He asked if we'd be willing to tour the Mediterranean on behalf of Operation Enduring Freedom. This meant being gone for Christmas and from our son.

Don came into our lives when Jay was three years old. As road musicians, job travel wasn't new for our family. Still, there were two things I was fighting as a traveling and working mother. The first was guilt at leaving our son on an important family holiday and second, peace of mind that we weren't damaging his psyche for life by being gone during this time. For the sake of my family, Don and I needed to manage this well so we all could cope successfully.

Sitting down at our kitchen table, I took a sip of cold coffee, "We've always been home for Christmas," I said to Don biting my bottom lip. I continued, "I don't know if touring is the right thing to do." Don scratched his head and nodded, "I'm not sure what to do either."

The November morning was passing fast. The Pentagon needed an answer by noon. "Mom," I called her anxiously with the news. "Dina, just GO," she said in her grade school principal voice, "you're doing something important for our military personnel by bringing music from home, especially during the holidays. Celebrate before you leave. Jay will be fine with me." I felt a small measure of comfort.

We had an early Christmas Eve party the Saturday before we left to perform for those serving in Operation Enduring Freedom. A fun evening on a much smaller scale, it still didn't make us feel better. For the next two days, there was a collective sadness over our house as we all prepared to pack and leave our home for the holidays. I hoped Jay would find the notes we left in his backpack in between the calls home that we would make, reminders that we were still with him in spirit. The band traveled across the Mediterranean by military ferry, arriving just in time for Christmas Eve dinner. The navy mess hall with its laminated floors and grey concrete walls was located on the U.S. Navy base in Sardinia, Italy. The base served as a logistical and technical center for submarine changeovers in the Mediterranean Sea.

Cheap red and green paper garlands were strung haphazardly around the room, like no one really cared about the holiday ambiance, but had to try. A silver, slightly tilted, tinsel Christmas tree with an assortment of holiday decorations hanging by threads served as our stage backdrop. Yet, there was still a drab vibe to the room.

Moving across the makeshift stage on the hard-cold floors of the mess hall, I began to sing in a low sultry voice "I'll be home for Christmas, you can count on me"... the noise of the clanking forks and knives against the aluminum trays began to stop. A sea of faces looked up from their Christmas dinners of sliced ham, turkey, brown gravy, mash potatoes, stuffing, and cranberry sauce. As each man looked up from his plate, I knew I was hitting an emotional touchstone. "I'll be home for Christmas...if only in my dreams..." from somber expressions, the countless seamen seated on neat rows of metal tables and chairs settled into wistful looks. I felt their yearning and pushed on with the song. I missed home too.

Once back home we heard, "Hey, Mom and Don! " Jay gave us a big hug as we came in the door, dragging tiredly from our long overseas flight. Just as fast as we got his hug, Jay was quickly out the front door with his bat slung over his shoulder and worn out baseball glove on his hand. He was heading to Freshman practice. Don and I stared at each other in surprise. In the end, we all adjusted and survived Christmas, and our son clearly carried on without us.

Having to travel for business as a parent can be a challenge, as it interrupts family routines and important traditions. Asking for support from our family and doing our best to have a bit of family Christmas before we left didn't alleviate our sadness, but these practices did support our son being able to move on with his normal routine, making our homecoming much sweeter. Coping with a family loss is never easy, but it does teach you the courage to move forward, even in the worst situations. Losses come in all kinds of unexpected moments.

My Father's Death

Losing a loved one while at work can be devastating. You not only have to deal immediately with one of life's worst possibilities, but you still must function in a professional environment. Learning to deal with grief and not shutting down is a powerful weapon against succumbing to despair.

In 1990, Don and I decided to return to Phoenix. My dad offered us his home as a place to get restarted. It was great stability for our little family. It provided a sense of steadiness for all of us, but especially Jay who, at five, needed to get off the road and start kindergarten. It also allowed me to finish what I had started long ago in San Francisco, going back to college.

As my dad aged, his health started to deteriorate, though he would never let us do much to help him. With a triple by-pass, diabetes, and debilitating arthritis, my dad suffered physically. He would eat and drink all the wrong foods; his diabetic condition would worsen, and he would slip into hypoglycemia episodes of confusion. When he would come out of the episodes at the hospital, he'd give us a sheepish grin promising to eat better, not drink and take his medications properly. But he continued to live the life he wanted, and he never complained. He didn't like men who complained, not surprising for an army veteran of the South Korean war.

My pocket buzzed while the sun was setting low on the Southwestern Sonoran Desert, changing the Saguaro cactus to auburn as their shadow elongated on the desert floor. The band was waiting for the first of three buses filled with corporate tourists to strike their first note. I pulled out my cell phone; it was my brother calling.

"I'm going on stage, what"? I said, irritated. "Dad's back at the hospital again," my brother replied. "What?" I whispered with concern. "A coma?" I said as I choked back my tears. I looked at my watch and did a quick calculation. With no one to take my place, it would be at least four hours before Don and I could get to the 7th Avenue Veteran's hospital located in the heart of the busy Phoenix district.

I gathered every ounce of courage I had, right down to my gut. It was the type of strength you wrench from deep inside when you are holding your full body weight in a plank position for more than a minute, while your stomach insists on trembling. You must hold tight, or you'll never make it. I went on autopilot and pushed through. Every song sung was one step closer to being finished and getting into the car to get to the hospital.

When we were finally on our way, important life moments with my dad started to flash through my mind. My quinceañera to celebrate my 15th birthday and coming out party, Dad walking with me down to Fisherman's Wharf to watch me perform, the birth of my son, his support of Don, his pride at my college graduation even though I was already 32. Funny, I only remembered the good times, and when my memories stopped, I knew my dad's spirit had passed.

"Dina," Don grabbed my hand while he was driving, I came back to attention.

"I think Dad has already passed," I said, and I started to cry. Don pushed the gas pedal to the floor and pulled me to him.

When we arrived at the VA hospital, my brothers and uncle were waiting. Your father is on life support the doctor told me. A blood clot has ruptured his intestine, gangrene set in and we can't save him. We all agreed that my dad was not the kind of man who would want to be on life support. Once removed, his heart stopped beating for good. I was grateful I was able to be with my family and kiss my father before he passed.

Grief and sadness can be a formidable influence. As entertainers, we don't have the luxury of taking bereavement leave or stopping a performance to address family issues. As they say, the show must go on, and it's true.

While I wanted to shut down during my father's passing, by focusing on job responsibilities, my mind temporarily shifted from the distress. To this day, I find comfort in working when I'm troubled. It allows me to bring in familiar tasks or normalcy into stressful situations that help to calm me down. While pushing through doesn't remove the pain, it keeps you moving forward by staying purposeful beyond sadness and grief.

Loss is a part of life. We need time to grieve the loss, but equally important is finding a way to move forward. Being able to cope with loss can also be a catalyst for new beginnings and life direction.

Dina and her Father, 1978

Heartcore Tips

Chapter 14: Overcoming Professional and Personal Loss

1. In stressful life situations, accept the challenge and look for the resources to make a new plan. Don't be afraid to seek out help or guidance and get back out there.
2. As working and traveling parents, keep home routines as normal as possible to help reduce the anxiety family members may feel because of your absence.
3. Leaving notes and other items between phone calls remind your loved ones that you are still with them.
4. When ready, focusing on work, tasks, and other responsibilities can serve as a distraction and bridge to new routines during times of grief.

#deospeaks

CHAPTER 15

Giving Back

The big red heart on the amphitheater screen was filling up with smaller red hearts. Like raindrops falling in a bucket with each donor's name, guests quickly texted their gifts for the homeless women's shelter. Don, the band, and I stood on stage playing crescendos every time a donation dropped into the heart to intensify the drama and encourage larger donations. A single drum roll or piano run accompanied small donations, while substantial donations got the whole band to play the Olympic Fanfare or Space Odyssey theme complete with timpani drum effects.

"Remember, any of the Dina Preston Band songs purchased tonight through their band app will be donated one-hundred percent to the foundation," the Master of Ceremonies prompted the audience, and on cue, we started playing our song "Where is She."

Immediately cell phones came out of tuxedo pockets and sparkling evening bags that resembled crown jewels. Their phones emitting blue light, the guests were busy tapping on their screens to access our app, purchasing our songs to support a great cause. That evening the non-profit raised over $80,000. We like to think we helped their bottom line.

With access to our band app, clients can raise money for their nonprofit events through our original music, while making the Dina Preston Band visible to potential new clients. As a direct marketing channel, we can quickly update our customers on band updates, booking information, and new music. As one of the up and coming groups of people with disposable incomes, we've learned that millennials will often switch brands to support a cause they feel is worthy. They will promote your brand quickly on social media if there is an emotional connection to a cause they support.

Dina Preston Band, Maricopa Veteran's Music Fest 2019
Courtesy of Justin Balczak

Community Colleges

I also enjoy giving back by sharing my school of hard knocks, street knowledge, and successes, along with my academic training in business. With a diverse population of students, community colleges across the nation are the entry or re-entry point for adults and students who can't afford or may not have the skills to attend a university. Many of my students are the first in their families to attend college. As a college professor, my students inspire me every day.

I heard a determined knock on my office door and looked up from my essay grading. "Dr. Ortiz," the student said in a bit of a panic, "I just lost my job, and I can't find one anywhere. I'm a single mom, and I need to start a business from home fast," she said, fighting back her tears.

"Come in," I said gently to the student in the ill-fitting t-shirt, holey jeans, and sockless Converse sneakers. I wasn't surprised when, in 2008, my student shared her economic struggles, the recession was hitting all of us. Many more students followed, all looking to start their own businesses quickly.

I had searched for a small business program in our college district but surprisingly was unable to find a path that would teach students the essentials of business start-up planning quickly. Thinking about my own journey as a small business owner, I reached out to my college colleagues who also owned small businesses with the idea of how to help our students quickly. We developed a Small Business Start-Up Certificate that could be completed in a year. Once approved, we reached out to our community and partnered with a local women's nonprofit to teach and work with their clients. This program has been growing strong for 8 years. The curriculum gives women the tools to start the initial stages or improve current businesses with courses in marketing, internet business, finance and taxes, staffing, and finally, how to write a business plan. I am also proud to share that the program won the Maricopa Community College Diversity (MCCCD) Award of Excellence. Recently the Federal Correctional Institute contacted me with interest regarding incorporating our Small Business Start-Up certificate into their adult continuing education programs.

By using an entrepreneurial method, we were able to meet a need in the community quickly, even in an economic environment of uncertainty. How? First, we listened to the needs of our students clearly and started from the bottom up. We looked at our current resources and identified key activities that supported the creation of a new small business start-up certificate we could offer quickly. Then we figured out the key partners to better leverage the economy of scale. This was an occupational, not a university transfer certificate, so long-term enrollment had to be addressed if the program was to survive. Partnering with a nonprofit allowed us to reach a student base outside our own zip code. It also meant a readymade student base complete with scholarships to cover the cost of student tuition. By considering all interactions in our network instead of just a narrow approach we were able to serve a much greater need.

Giving back is rewarding professionally and personally. It makes us think beyond our own needs by considering the impact we can make in our communities one person, one event, and one need at a time. Giving back offers positive changes for those who are giving and receiving.

The Maricopa Community Colleges' Diversity Advisory Council
is proud to present the 2013 DAC Award of Excellence to

"Fresh Start Women's Foundation"
Dr. Dina Preston-Ortiz, Reyes Medrano, Dr. Sue VanBoven, Roxanne Ruiz, Norma Chandler and Dominic Bartola

Paradise Valley Community College
in recognition of outstanding efforts on behalf of diversity and inclusion at the Maricopa Community Colleges.

April 10, 2013

Dr. Rufus Glasper, Chancellor | Nikki Jackson, Vice-Chancellor HR
DAC Co-chair | Dr. Shouan Pan, President MCC
DAC Co-chair

Small Business Start-Up Certificate
Maricopa Community College's Diversity Advisory Council (DAC)
Award of Excellence

Heartcore Tips:
Chapter 16: Giving Back

1. A socioeconomic approach to business recognizes that by taking care of the community in which the business functions, the community, in turn, will take care of the business.
2. Use an entrepreneurial method to develop ideas from the ground up. Working backward identifies key activities that align with the end goal.
3. Look for key partners to leverage economy of scales.

#deospeaks

CHAPTER 16

Live to Ride

"Now boarding Group A, one through thirty," the Southwest Airlines ticket agent announces over the intercom. I look apologetically at Don.

I forgot to reserve our boarding passes yesterday as I promised. With assigned section C, thirty through sixty, we'll be the last group to board on our way to Washington, D.C. and will not sit together on the long flight. As we board the Boeing 737, I'm still hoping Don; his rich sounding acoustic guitar made from Koa wood and I can find a seat together on the plane. After 30 years, I still want Don and his guitar by my side.

Dina just completed her tenure as Business/IT Division Chair at her college, another tentacle she seemed to integrate easily into her multifaceted skill set. We were just in Orlando, where I proudly watched her receive the American Association of Community Colleges Dale P. Parnell Faculty Distinction Recognition. Dr. D, as her students nicknamed her, was one of only twenty-two college professors to receive this national award in 2019. No surprise. I watched her take thirty-one cents, her passion and talent for music and turn it into a multifaceted career, that has spanned over many continents.

To celebrate, Don and I are heading to Washington D.C. to spend time with good friends we met many years ago along our global journey. Don's warmth and love of people, along with his dedication to creating a memorable and joyful customer experience seems to transform clients into lifelong friends, helping us maintain important relationships authentically.

"Don, what's going on up there," said Dina. Walking along the magnificent National Mall lined with ancient oaks and maple trees, littered with lazy families floundering on the lush green lawn, Don and I are thoroughly enjoying our stroll through the nation's capital as we watch young couples zip by on the hottest new mode of transportation, lime green scooters. Looking up, I see the commotion ahead. Standing in clusters by the hundreds, in their dark blue wool uniforms and checkerboard ribbons just above the brim of their caps, we have stumbled onto hundreds of Chicago police who had gathered on the steps of the State Capital to honor those killed in the line of duty. There is an air of brotherhood we understand all too well. Much like the military, only the strongest choose these honorable and challenging career paths. These men and women are the true stars in our song the "Field of Blue". Stopping to take in the majesty of Lincoln's Memorial, Don and I reflect. As I read President Lincoln's second inauguration speech on the marble walls, it's easy to visualize his determination. He did not let adversity discourage him during our nation's struggles. Instead, he focused on providing excellence over perfection, doing the right thing, and keeping his end game in mind. Even with mistakes and major setbacks, President Lincoln kept operations moving by optimizing his talent and resources to bring about the reconciliation of the union and freedom for all American citizens. It's a good reminder of the importance of staying true to your internal compass and values.

Don and Dina in Washington D.C. 2019

On the way home, we detour to Austin, Texas, to see our son for a few days in a city bustling with IT startup companies working to make their version of the American dream come true. With its "All Dogs Are Created Equal" provocative wall graffiti, a perfect mixture of country meets hippy music scene, a social and politically diverse population, with unbelievable food in the middle of the U.S. conservative heartland, Austin business leaders are finding their own competitive advantages by disrupting the status quo. Our son is working in one of these bootstrap startups, creating new income streams globally through technology by successfully navigating cross culture competencies required when your staff is a half a globe away.

The buzz of the alarm goes off at 3:00 am so we can catch our final plane home from this beautiful break. Throwing back the cover from the bed in our son's apartment to get ready to go, I have to admit to myself that Dina is looking more tired than usual.

"Don, check out my arms, they are riddled with red hives and blotches," Dina pokes me apprehensively as we land into Sky Harbor International Airport. By the evening she is covered in raised red welts with a swollen throat.

Her fever is 103. The red spots have now swelled into a continuously raised rash covering most of her body. With swollen lymph nodes, Dina now looks like a burn patient struggling to breathe. With a tense body, my heart starts to race as I wrap her in a blanket and get her loaded in the car. I try not to think of the worse as she hyperventilates, shivers, and moans.

"Don," Dina looks up from the emergency room bed with glassy red eyes, "my black jeans, boots and white cowboy shirt are still hanging in the closet, put them in the truck in case they release me so that I can go to the gig tonight." Then she closes her eyes and is out of it. The emergency room doctor comes in and immediately starts an I.V. drip while the nurse works to bring down Dina's temperature. I can't believe (actually, I can) that Dina is still trying to figure out how to get to our Harley Davidson Corporate gig tonight.

By the afternoon Dina is transferred by ambulance to the hospital. She is in stable condition, but the doctor wants to observe her overnight to watch her infection and white blood cell count that is elevated to fifteen.

Now that Dina's condition is steady, I start to assess the business situation. I call my music friends to see if anyone can stop by to sit in tonight, but it's too last minute. Everyone is already booked. It's up to me. I have to get the Dina Preston Band through the gig successfully without Dina Preston. First time in 29 years, 43 countries and 26 global tours that Dina has ever missed a gig. I stay focused on my job responsibilities by falling back into my normal gig routine to help keep me going.

Steel and chrome hogs, fat boys and road kings with their own painted stories in vivid custom colors of red, blue and black, gleam against the Harley Davidson neon marquee. Bandana covered heads decked in black shirts and boots are still riding into the event. It's going to be a full house; bombshell blondes with deep southwestern tans, tats, and long leather boots grace the patio in their American flag tank tops, waiting for the Dina Preston Band. Under a stage of crimson-blue lights, I turn to the band and whisper, "vamp on A, swing blues," and announce in my MC voice...

"Hey everybody.... welcome to Harley Davidson of Scottsdale..."

EPILOGUE

Today, we are running our music business in a very different world than when we began in 1989. Technology has both enhanced and disrupted the way business is conducted. With a more competitive landscape, it's never been more essential to understand how technology and marketing can leverage your distinct competencies to improve your bottom line. We keep learning and applying. We can't wait to share our continued travels and new business insights with you.

Wishing you many blessings,
Dina and Don

FIELD OF BLUE MISSION

Please Join the Discussion

If you enjoyed learning the unique art and strategy to increasing profit and making innovative and strategic choices all while keeping relationships, family, dreams, and passion alive through Dina and Don's unique work with the U.S. military, State Department and Fortune 500 companies, here are some ideas on how to share our adventures and tips.

- Share your business insights and discuss the book with other readers at https://www.facebook.com/DinaPrestonBand/
- Share **31Cents to 43 Countries, Hardcore Tips to Increasing Profits** with your managers, employees, associations, networking group, friends, veterans, active military personnel, a college student, colleague, or executive.
- Donate **31Cents to 43 Countries, Hardcore Tips to Increasing Profits**, in paperback to veteran centers, workforce development centers, college and university classrooms. The precious gift of knowledge, coupled with exceptional life experiences, can change the

lives of those willing to learn, along with their families and communities.

- If you are on social media, share a bit about the book and how it touched you along with a link to the e-book. Contact your favorite media podcast or radio host to have Dina and Don share their life-changing stories in person. Today, because of access to technology, listeners are potent resources for media content.
- Host a reading and concert followed by a VIP meet and greet with greenroom photo access to Dina, Don and the Band.
- Share updated news on the **Dina Preston Band Field of Blue Mission** and **Show with Meeting and Event Planners, Destination Management Companies, Fundraiser, Concert Promoters, Event Planners, and Organizers.**

For information about having Dina and Don speak or hold business workshops at your next meeting or special event, or to have the Dina Preston Band entertain at your next event, please contact DEO Entertainment Group at (623) 330.0267 or by email at: deoentertainmentgroup@gmail.com.

www.dinaprestonband.com

www.deospeaks.com

APPENDIX A

Front Line News: Man, I Feel Like A Women

The Frontline News

Soldiers sing with Dina Preston Band

Casey Craig
Volunteer
Spc. Mason T. Lowery

Lt. Col. Eric Schwartz,1st Battalion, 64th Armor commander, Maj. Michael Donovan, 1/64 Armor S-3, and Capt. Warren Sponsler, 1/64 Armor S-4, sing Shania Twain's "I feel like a woman" with singer Dina Preston and guitarist Don Ortiz during a USO concert Jan. 10 at Camp Pennsylvania, Kuwait.

Spc. Mason T. Lowery
50th PAD

Soldiers sing with Dina Preston Band

Soldiers took a break from training and maintaining
to let loose and blow off some steam with
The Dina Preston Band Jan. 10.
The band brought their mix of blues, country and rock 'n 'roll to the soldiers at Camp
Pennsylvania for a USO concert.
Rather than just sing to the soldiers, Dina

APPENDIX B

Royal Embassy of Saudi Arabia, Washington, D.C. (Death Document)

١٩٩٥/١/١٧م

أقر هنا بأنه خلال إقامتي في المملكة العربية السعودية سوف التزم بكافة قوانينها وأنظمتها وتقاليــدها والآداب. نشرعية مع مراعاة قيم المجتمع السعودي واحترام تقاليده ومشاعره وعدم ادخال الممنوعات والمنـــشورات. او الكتب والاشرطة التي تتعارض مع أديان الاسلامي ، وعدم تنظيم تجمعات او الاشتراك فيها. او الدعــوة لأي مذهب ديني او سياسي. كما قني على علم تام بأن لمواد المسكرة والعقاقير المخدرة والمطبوعات المخلــــة بالآداب العامة وجميع المطبوعات الدينية والسياسية ممنوعة من دخول المملكة العربية السعودية. سواء كانـــت للاستعمال الشخصي او خلافه – وان عقوبة تهريب المخدرات الى المملكة او ترويجها داخلها ، هي القتــل – كما قني على علم تام بأن مخالفتي لقوانين وأنظمة المملكة العربية السعودية سيعرضني للجزاء.

I hereby certify that, during my stay in Saudi Arabia, I shall abide by all the laws and regulations
of the kingdom and I shall respect the morals, customs, values and feelings of Saudi society. I
also should not smuggle in any prohibited items. I am aware that alcohol, drug narcotics, porno-
graphic materials and all types of religious, political or cultural leaflets, pamphlets, magazines,
books, audio tapes, video tapes, films, or other references of all sorts, contradictory to Islam are
prohibited from entering the Kingdom of Saudi Arabia, whether for personal use or otherwise.
I should not participate in or call for gatherings, whether for sectarian, religious or political
purposes. Any types of illegal drugs and narcotics smuggling in and distribution inside the
Kingdom of Saudi Arabia is punishable by DEATH.
I agree that, if I am convicted because of violation of the laws and regulations of the Kingdom
of Saudi Arabia, I shall be subject to penalty.

I HAVE READ AND UNDERSTOOD THE ABOVE STATEMENT:

PRINT NAME   _____

SIGNATURE   _____

الرقم : ١/٥٠١   التاريخ : ٧٥/٤/٨ هـ   المرافق : ١٤ هـ   المرفقات : ١٩م

APPENDIX C

Dina Preston Band Client Review

Client Review

Gig 295687 - submitted by Rabbine H

On a scale of 1 to 5 (1=lowest, 5=highest), how would you rate The Dina Preston Band in terms of their **professionalism**? Score: 5

On a scale of 1 to 5 (1=lowest, 5=highest), how **accommodating** was The Dina Preston Band in handling special requests for your event? Score: 5

On a scale of 1 to 5 (1=lowest, 5=highest), how would you rate The Dina Preston Band in terms of their **overall talent**? Score: 5

On a scale of 1 to 5 (1=lowest, 5=highest), how strongly would you **recommend** The Dina Preston Band to a friend? Score: 5

And finally, on a scale of 1 to 5 (1=lowest, 5=highest), how would you rate your **overall satisfaction** with The Dina Preston Band? Score: 5

Additional Comments:
Simply put in 3 words, the Dina Preston Band was sensational, dynamic and AWESOME!!!! A mix of country, pop, rock and patriotic songs earned them a well deserved standing ovation. The U.S.Marines from Twenty-Nine Palms and Camp Pendleton sang with Dina on stage creating a legend on film that is being seen on military bases in Iraq and worldwide uplifting the spirits of deployed soldiers. The audience was roaring with laughter! Dina Preston is a tremendously talented vocalist with a beautiful and clear voice. Dina and Don are a rare combination of musical talent, enthusiasm and humor!!!

Response (optional)

If you would like to respond to the client, please do so here. You may leave a note to simply say "Thanks" or reply to any specific comments you would like to address. Please be professional in your response as it will be published on the GigMasters website and viewed by future clients. Your response may have up to 675 characters.

Cover illustration and cover design by Francajoez
Author photograph by www.tzenphoto.com

ACKNOWLEDGMENTS

This book would not have been possible without the critical feedback and support of many people. While I knew writing a book would be no easy task, I had no idea the joys and frustrations nine rewrites would bring. Don and I want to thank our book coach, Mark Mikelat and content coach Maya Luna Cristobel, for sharing their talent and knowledge with us. Special kudos to our reading team who took time out of their busy schedules to review the first draft of our book and offer their feedback, Robert Keith, Brian Quarles, and David Aldridge. All of you made essential and unique contributions in helping us tell our story, and we are forever grateful.

ENDNOTES

i. The Multinational Force & Observers (n.d.). About. Retrieved from http://mfo. org/en/about-us

ii. Nieves, E. (2018, April 4). The 'Endless War' of Land Mines in the Balkans. New York Times. Retrieved from https://www.nytimes. com/2018/04/04/lens/theendless-war-of-land-mines-in-the-balkans.html

iii. T. Finerty, personal communication, October 6, 2006

iv. Diyarbakir, A Journey in Time (n.d.). Retrieved May 1, 2019 from https://hometurkey.com/en/destinations/diyarbakir

v. Williamson, W. (1995, October 8). U.S. TROOPS IN MACEDONIA DOING

vi. STRANGE, NEW JOB OF PEACEKEEPING. Chicano Tribune. Retrieved from https://www.chicagotribune.com/news/ct-xpm-1995-10-08-9510080353-story. html

vii. Wafa Waheed, A. & Gall, C. (2007, Feb 28). A Mile from Cheney, Afghan Bomber Kills at Least 23. Asia Pacific. New York Times. Retrieved January 5, 2019 from https://www.nytimes.com/2007/02/28/world/asia/28cheney.html

viii. United States of America v. Richard Colvin a/k/a Abdul Raheem, Abu, (18 U.S.C.

ix. §2332a(a) (1) -(United States District Court District of Massachusetts, 2002) Retrieved January 7, 2018 from https://fas.org/irp/news/2002/01/reidindictment.pdf

x. Sweeney, C. (2008, June 9). Red Tape, bribes greet small business in Russia. *Reuters.* Retrieved January 11, 2019 from https://www.reuters. com/article/us-russia-smallbusiness/red-tape-bribes-greet-small-business-inrussia-idUSL2645065620080610

xi. Mourningthe Lossof Johnny Grant, Honorary Mayorof Hollywood: Congressional Record-House. (2008, January 15) (Testimony of Ms. WATSON) Retrieved on

xii. January 13, 2019 from https://www.govinfo.gov/content/pkg/CREC-2008-01-15/ pdf/CREC-2008-01-15-pt1-PgH7-3.pdf

xiii. United States Department of Labor (2019). Women in the Labor Force in 2010. Women's Bureau. Retrieved January 13, 2019 from https://www.dol.gov/wb/factsheets/qf-laborforce-10.htm

INDEX

R

S

T

www.ingramcontent.com/pod-product-compliance
Lightning Source LLC
Chambersburg PA
CBHW060921040426
42445CB00011B/724